S0-CFW-088

Name: SUSAN SOBBOTT
Job Title: PRESIDENT, OPEN FROM AMERICAN EXPRESS
Joined: 1990

Why did OPEN from American Express create a book on how to grow a small business? Aren't there already endless resources available to entrepreneurs? In fact, there are so many resources that it can be a daunting task to find the information you need when you need it, it becomes even more of an issue when you are pressed for time.

To provide concise and actionable information to help you grow your business, that's why we developed the OPEN Book.

It's that simple, and so is the information you'll find inside. Covering everything from building your Web site to managing your credit, the book is full of practical tips and advice — the layout is equally straightforward. There are no cluttered graphics or flashy headlines, no ads to divert your attention.

The Book also gave us a chance to share the inspiration we constantly find in our OPEN customers. We have included profiles of six of our Cardmembers whose stories embody the passion and dedication of every entrepreneur — innovators and trendsetters, they disclose some of the lessons they've learned along the way that helped them grow their businesses. They are on the cutting edge of new developments in small

business — from retirees embarking on a new phase in their professional life to passionate individuals who weave social consciousness into their bottom line.

Twenty years ago, American Express was among the first companies to recognize the force that small businesses represent in our economy — over 99% of all firms in the U.S. are small businesses — and to create products and services to meet your unique needs. Today, OPEN is the team at American Express dedicated exclusively to serving small businesses, not only by providing valuable payment products, but also by providing resources to help you grow your business. *OPENforum.com,* a new online portal that provides insights from expert business owners and opportunities for networking, is yet another tool to encourage and support you in your business success.

Your stories and suggestions continue to inspire us to innovate and to evolve as we seek to serve you better. It is our deepest privilege to be associated with you and to help you bring your ideas to life.

Thank you for your business, and I hope you enjoy the Book!

Edited and Produced by

Winkreative
Suite 632
611 Broadway
New York, NY
10012
www.winkreative.com

Creative Director —
TYLER BRÛLÉ

Managing Editor —
JENNIFER McALEAR

Editor —
SAUL TAYLOR

Art Director —
KEN LEUNG

Designer —
BEN ROBERTSON

Photo Editors —
STEPHEN LEDGER-LOMAS
ROSE PERCY

Production Editor —
JACQUELINE DEACON

Sub-editors —
THOMAS CALVOCORESSI
BRIAN HEALY

Editorial Assistant —
DIANA KEH

Account Director, Winkreative —
MEIGHAN DOBSON

For OPEN from American Express —
AMY FITZGIBBONS
PATRICIA SHORES
MARCELLA SHINDER

OFFICE PACE

IN THE PAST TWO DECADES, THE WORKPLACE HASN'T JUST CHANGED — IT'S COMPLETELY EVOLVED

There was a time, although it's hard to believe it now, before the Internet. A time when the landline telephone ruled the desk, when letters were written on actual paper, when a secretary took down messages and a pocket calculator did the math. Some remember it fondly: a simpler time, before the mighty Information Superhighway bulldozed its way through the reams of paper. In two short decades, the workplace has become a different kind of techno-jungle.

Now we are all reliant on gadgets, and on instant, high-speed access to the Internet; thousands even use the Internet as their sole medium of trade. It has been a similar story for many other workplace tools. In 20 years, the way we work has changed faster than most of us can believe.

Back in 1987, the office was a perforated paper trail. All communication and organization was about paper. "In" and "Out" trays were our only communications vessels; all appointments and contacts were tidied into large leather ring-bound organizers; and the stationery cupboard was filled with staplers, paper clips, floppy disks, rubber stamps and hole punches.

Until the early '90s, you were still tied to your phone or your computer by a spaghetti of wires. And then came the cell phone. By the mid-'90s, Motorola StarTACs, Apple Newtons and other portable digital organizers suddenly shrank the office down to handheld proportions. Innovation in technology has followed suit.

As the speed and reliability of our accessories improved, so did the usefulness of the Internet — it became an integral part of work life, multiplying productivity and facilitating the way business is done. E-commerce changed the world of work beyond recognition. Combined with the laptop, hot-desking seemed the only way to go.

Although it hasn't happened quite as predicted, our desks are still becoming so hot that we are finding ourselves less likely to sit at them. From desktop answerphones to Voice over Internet Protocol (VoIP), from fax machines to online networking and virtual banking, work life is merging with home life. The whole lot can now be conducted and stored from a virtual desktop anywhere in the world and at any time of the day.

Still yearning for the old days?

Text: **Henrietta Thompson**
Photography: **Metz + Racine**

1987–1991

HARD CELL
For the very early adopters, a cell phone such as the
Nokia Mobira Cityman or the Motorola DynaTAC is
an impressive accessory to flash around the office.

1987　　　　1988　　　　1989　　　　1990　　　　1991

DOES NOT COMPUTE
The introduction of personal computers to the
office means that workers have extra time to
go through their in-tray in the morning,
while they wait for the machine to boot up.

FILING SYSTEM
If you happen to be a high-flying yuppie,
being organized is the key: Everyone wants
a ring-bound agenda, the latest innovation
in organizing your life.

1991–1995

HAND-HELD

The first generation handheld computers arrive in
the workplace, allowing users to schedule their
appointments and write documents — complete
with early handwriting recognition software.

1991	1992	1993	1994	1995

TAUPE OF THE RANGE

The only acceptable color for workplace electronics is
beige, embodied perfectly by your Mac Classic. You'll
have to wait till '98 and the introduction of the iMac
before any injection of color.

FLIP OUT

Fitting perfectly in your pocket, the Motorola
StarTAC wearable cell phone is the smallest,
lightest and most popular "ready to wear"
accessory yet. Its flip-up cover is also a first.

1995–1999

SEARCH LIGHT
The AltaVista search engine is launched, and —
as the first searchable, full-text database of a large
part of the World Wide Web — goes on to surpass
other search engines in popularity.

1995   1996   1997   1998   1999

LAP IT UP
Laptop computers become popular among
business people in the mid-'90s, and when
Microsoft introduces Windows 95, compact
portability becomes increasingly available.

E-REVOLUTION
Amazon.com, one of the first global
e-commerce sites, perseveres even
when the dot-com bubble bursts and many
e-companies go out of business.

1999–2003

GLOBAL MARKETPLACE
eBay, founded in 1995, is now a global phenomenon, launching its physical outlets, eBay stores, in 2002, and opening up e-commerce to more than 200 million shoppers worldwide.

SUPER-PRODUCTIVE
Coffee, vitamins, jellybeans: Whatever the supplement, office workers need the boost more than ever as they struggle to keep up with technology and the new possibilities it affords.

MOBILITY MATTERS
Cell phones are featuring more and more in office life, with the big players such as Nokia and Motorola launching as many as five phones globally a year.

2003–2007

SECOND SIGHT
With a second generation of Internet-based services, so-called Web 2.0, the office finds a fifth dimension through community-based Web sites such as Second Life, YouTube, Adsense and Digg.

2003   2004   2005   2006   2007

CHAT ONLINE
Since the introduction of Voice over Internet Protocol services in 2004, Skype and others are changing the way we view the phone and telecommunications. Simplicity rules.

BERRY EASY
The ultra-slim BlackBerry® Pearl™ brings e-mail on the move to more people than ever since the original device's launch. Addictive and ergonomic, users are in touch at all times.

BUSINESS CLASS

FROM BUYING PREGNANT ALPACAS AND HARLEY-DAVIDSONS TO FUNDING SURGICAL START-UPS AND BAKERIES, HERE IS A COLORFUL COLLECTION OF SMALL BUSINESS PERSONALITIES

What do you think of when you think of a small business? Maybe words like agility, flexibility and innovation spring to mind. But for many of the businesses profiled on the following pages, size represents a more fundamental freedom: the freedom to be themselves and the chance to take control of their own destinies. They're "coolpreneurs," corporate workers who've decided to go it alone; "baby-boomer-preneurs," retirees who've opted to start a new chapter in their working lives; "mompreneurs," mothers who've found new and fulfilling ways to meld their working and personal lives; and "ethicalpreneurs," those who've aimed to use their business as a platform to influence or effect social change.

Innovative business models such as these are leading the way in the New Economy — one that hinges on technology and competition in an increasingly global marketplace, but also one that's built on passion, resourcefulness and a determination to throw out the old rule-book — or even write a new one. "There weren't many precedents for what we're doing," says Connie Betts, who gave up the lucrative world of software design to open an alpaca farm.

"We didn't read business journals or have five-year plans; in other words, we kind of made it up as we went along."

That can-do attitude may be as old as America itself, but today's entrepreneurs are finding their own ways of following their dreams. "We knew we had a great idea," says Jeff Brown, co-founder of Harley-Davidson–rental company Eagle Rider. "We were so determined to make it work, we'd have slept on the floor if we had to. We thought, 'If we don't do it now we're never going to. And whatever happens, it will certainly be a great learning experience.'"

That mixture of leap-in-the-dark faith and dauntless enthusiasm is key to the success of all the following entrepreneurs. Society may change and economies may boom and bust, but the spirit of adventure that drives the small business pioneer remains one of the eternal verities. No wonder corporate giants can only look on in awe or envy as the latest left-field start-up races through the field to capture the public imagination. It's incontrovertible proof, if any were needed, that small is not just big. It's also beautiful.

Name:	CHRIS McINTYRE & JEFF BROWN
Company:	EAGLE RIDER
Industry:	TOURISM
Location:	LOS ANGELES, CA

Eagle Rider's slogan is "We rent dreams." And a quick glance around their Los Angeles headquarters soon makes clear what kind of desires they're purveying. There are racks stacked with bandannas, leather jackets, cut-off denims and other "outlaw wear." Route 66 signs jostle for space alongside vintage gas pumps and mammoth Stars and Stripes. Led Zeppelin and Steppenwolf alternate on the sound system.

And then there are the bikes. Through a side door, you'll find an Aladdin's cave of gleaming Harley-Davidsons of every stripe — the Fat Boy, the Low Rider, the Electra Glide (in blue, no less). Eagle Rider offers you the chance to unlock your inner Easy Rider and roar out of your workaday life down the highway to, if not Hell, then at least Death Valley or Palm Beach. "We give people a chance to live the American myth," says Eagle Rider co-founder Chris McIntyre. "The image

of the Harley and the open road is out there in the collective consciousness. We make it real."

Eagle Rider's success is a testament to the potency of that myth. McIntyre started the company with business partner Jeff Brown 13 years ago; at that time, they had four bikes (including their own) and were operating out of a garage in San Pedro. Today, they're the world's largest motorcycle-rental company, offering tours out of 40 rental outlets across America and Europe, with a fleet of 3,000 bikes and around 50,000 rentals a year. With an average daily rate of $75, they're now expanding beyond Harleys — not only to BMWs and Hondas, but also to jet skis, quad bikes and snow mobiles.

McIntyre and Brown are uniquely placed to share in the wish fulfillment they're offering. The idea for Eagle Rider came out of an aborted trip to Europe in 1992; the pair, both bike fanatics since childhood, and complementary business personalities — "Chris is more of a promotional person, while I prefer the anonymous administration role," says Brown, wryly — had planned to take sabbaticals from their jobs as AT&T executives to travel around the Continent on Harleys.

OPPOSITE
McIntyre and Brown hit the open road

RIGHT
Hector Martinez gives the bikes some T.L.C. at the Eagle Rider H.Q.

BELOW RIGHT
A small fraction of the Eagle Rider fleet

BELOW
The Eagle Rider motif

"Neither of us had bikes at that point, so we tried to rent them," recalls Brown. "We looked in the phone book, and there was nothing. We'd ask around, and people would end up asking us where they could rent Harleys in the U.S. So a light bulb went off in our heads. We saw a void in the market."

The pair jumped ship from corporate America — "we were so waiting for the right opportunity to do that," says McIntyre with a grin — and made their first "test rental" a year later, to a quartet of Austrians. "They went off on a 16-day trip through Bryce Canyon," says McIntyre, "and I remember wondering if we'd ever see them again. But when they came back, we could see they'd changed. One guy had tears in his eyes; he said that ever since he was a boy and he'd seen a poster of Elvis sitting on a Harley, it had symbolized the American dream for him. He was so moved. And we were getting goose bumps. We thought, 'Wow, we're really onto something here.'"

Even so, progress was slow, thanks to a little matter called liability insurance. It took two years before a contact in the mobile-home-rental business agreed to cover them — "we would have weekly meetings just for the

sake of meeting, even though there was no progress, just to keep up our spirits," recalls Brown — and they built their initial fleet by buying in bulk on credit from several Harley dealerships, as well as offering Harley enthusiasts the chance to buy new bikes and loan them to Eagle Rider for rent. "They got their money back in a couple of years," says McIntyre. "So we quickly grew to 50 bikes. That's when we opened the Los Angeles headquarters." Gesturing expansively, he adds, "As you can see, things grew pretty rapidly from there."

Today, Eagle Rider L.A. takes up a city-block-sized series of units. Bikes are lovingly serviced and buffed in one; the company's guided tours (with optional additions such as luggage-support vehicles and spare bikes) with titles like California Dreamin' (from $1,550 for 4-6 days) and Rocky Mountain High (from $3,200 for up to 15 days) are arranged in another. It's one of four company-owned stores; the rest — from Billings, Montana to Malaga, Spain — are franchises. McIntyre is keen to ensure that the ethos of the company is maintained as it grows, "We're purists in a lot of ways. We want to create a global company that still has a family feel."

Eagle Rider now employs about 400 people (including franchisees), and while McIntyre and Brown are coy about profits, they concede that they're "pretty healthy." Such success hasn't gone unnoticed by the vacation-industry conglomerates, but Eagle Rider's founders aren't overly keen to re-embrace corporate America just yet. "The beauty of a small business is that you can be nimble," says Brown. "Bureaucracy makes it difficult for huge corporations to act quickly or be flexible. And you can become dead men walking in corporate America with a lack of passion. We're incredibly passionate about what we do."

So passionate that, despite the fact they're now both family men, they can still be found out in the canyons on their own Harleys whenever they can get away, "We don't get out so often these days, though," laments Brown.

"But, when we do, it's all the sweeter," puts in McIntyre.

"And you say 'Oh yeah: This is the reason why people come to us,'" says Brown, beaming. "Because it's so much fun."

OPPOSITE
McIntyre and Brown take a pit stop

LEFT
Living the Eagle Rider dream in Malibu

ABOVE
Andy Wegener and Petra Louda, Eagle Rider's tour-group organizers

Name:	LENIE RAMOS
Company:	LITTLE TWIG
Industry:	BEAUTY
Location:	EL SEGUNDO, CA

If a small business is judged on its actual physical size, then Little Twig more than fits the bill. Its four employees work out of a tiny office in the funky L.A. neighborhood of El Segundo. It produces petite products for little customers — organic, extra-mild bubble baths, shampoos and washcloths designed specifically for babies. And then there's its C.E.O. Lenie Ramos is a diminutive 33-year-old who could pass as — and is frequently mistaken for — someone half her age. "People are always a little shocked that I'm the boss," she laughs. "I get a lot of people coming in and saying, 'What do you do here?' It's sometimes a little difficult for many traditional business guys to take on board."

But in its four-year existence, Little Twig has become one of the biggest tiny companies around. Its products are available in 450 stores worldwide, including the Whole Foods Market and Baby Style chains in the United States, and Bonza Brats in Australia. Last year Ramos sold nearly 30,000 bottles of foams, oils, potions and lotions to delighted moms, including several celebrity clients. "It's so exciting to see my things in stores," says Ramos, whose enthusiasm is infectious. "I sometimes can't resist adjusting the displays, bringing us to the front a little more." She beams. "I feel like I'm accomplishing something that's so real and tangible."

Ramos — the "Lenie" is short for Eleanor, "which I never go by" — was born in the U.S. to Filipino immigrant parents, who instilled a work ethic in her that she describes as "ferocious." Initially, this ferocity was channeled into a job as a graphic designer for TV title sequences; she spent nearly a decade refining her skills, and won an Emmy in 1999 as part of the team that worked on ESPN's X Games coverage. (She maintains her design skills by creating the user-friendly graphics — all toony bees, snails and ladybugs — that adorn Little Twig's products.) But despite her success, she felt that something was missing. "It was a kind of epiphany where I felt like I had no quality of life," she says, sitting behind a less-than-imposing desk at the twig-bedecked Little Twig headquarters. "Everyone works so hard in that industry — it's almost like a badge of honor to stay as late as possible — and I started asking myself what I was actually contributing to society."

Ramos decided the best way out of her ennui would be to start her own business. "I saw people around me doing it, and I thought it would push me out of my comfort zone, and, hopefully, make me a more well-rounded person, someone who's going to keep learning." She pauses and smiles. "I don't know about the well-rounded bit, but I sure have learned a lot."

Ramos's initial idea was to start a design-linked company, but her plans were up-ended when she had the bright idea of giving her infant niece a bottle of bubble bath for her birthday. "My sister said, 'Thanks, but she can't use this, she may get an infection,'" recalls Ramos. "And that set me to thinking, 'Well, how do other kids and parents manage?' That piqued my interest, and I went out and found that there were only a tiny number of safe and mild products for babies."

To a certain extent, Ramos was flying blind; she had no background in chemistry or formula-making — in fact, she says a little

sheepishly, she failed her school chemistry exam three times — and she was childless at the time. (Today, she has a year-old daughter who is "my first and best customer.") But she consulted pediatricians and parent friends, noted the "huge baby boom" of recent years and sensed an opportunity waiting to be seized. She set up a D.I.Y. research lab at home: "Our hallways were filled with gallons of lotion," she recalls, "and my husband told me, 'O.K., where are you going with this?'" The answer was an office, and an initial line of shampoos and bubble baths free of parabens, sulfates and mineral oils. "I started this whole thing with my own money," she says. "I had no initial investors. I guess there were precedents for what I was doing, like Anita Roddick with The Body Shop — I read up on her story — but it felt like a huge leap in the dark. I think what got us going was that we were incredibly focused: We were targeting zero-to-eights."

Other words are equally important to Ramos and Little Twig, "inclusive" and "organic" foremost among them. "It's really important to include parents and the wider

OPPOSITE
Ramos prepares gift packages in the Little Twig warehouse

BELOW
A sample of the Little Twig range

community in our development," she says. To that end, the company encourages feedback on its Web site and from callers: "That's not just lip service," says Ramos. "We've created a giant, virtual mom-and-baby group. But there's also the unexpected stuff. Our products aren't just for kids — I use them myself. But we got a call from a woman with cancer who said that our baby oil was the only product she could stand while she was undergoing chemotherapy. That's very rewarding." Little Twig also donates a portion of its profits to a different child-related charity each year; the current beneficiary is the Everychild Foundation, which helps children who suffer from disease, abuse, poverty or disability.

Little Twig's production finally went all-organic last year. "There are no pesticides or detergents in the products, and everything's from renewable resources," says Ramos. The company also uses biodegradable packaging and paper, as well as recyclable bottles; in fact, if you return four bottles to their offices, they offer 30 per cent off the next online purchase. "I'm more aware of what's at stake since I started this company and became a mother," says Ramos. "Having a child makes you aware they'll inherit what we leave behind us."

That's perhaps the most fundamental aspect of Ramos and Little Twig's innate smallness: Both owner and company want to do what they do without leaving a huge footprint (carbon or otherwise) on the world. "When I was thinking of the company name, I wanted something that felt natural and simple," says Ramos, glancing at a spray of boughs. "I wanted this company to be simple, from our ingredients to our packaging to our office to our whole operation." She smiles. "We don't need that much space. We just want to do a good and valuable job."

Name:	CONNIE & THOMAS BETTS
Company:	CASCADE ALPACAS
Industry:	FARMING
Location:	HOOD RIVER, OR

What's your idea of the perfect retirement? A long, leisurely cruise around the Caribbean? A condo in a gated community? For Connie and Thomas Betts, it's a ranch in Oregon's Hood River Valley. And 15 alpacas.

"Aren't they the sweetest things?" asks Thomas, as Zeus, Amadeus, Carmen, et al. lope over to greet us. It's a rhetorical question; the couple are keen to share their delight in these "sweet, hearty animals," as Connie calls them, with the hundreds of visitors who descend on their Cascade Alpacas ranch and attached Foothills Yarn & Fiber knitting supplies store every weekend.

The Bettses are emblematic of those 50-something baby boomers who are rewriting the rules of retirement by discovering their inner entrepreneur at an age when previous generations had begun to wind down; a recent analysis of U.S. government data found that those aged 55 to 64 represent one of the fastest-growing groups of self-employed workers. "We had had our careers," says Connie — she wrote high-tech programs for a software company while Thomas worked for a marine-supply firm — "but we wanted a fresh challenge. I guess we were the classic empty-nesters; the kids had gone off to college and we were dreaming of a more rural life and a fresh start." Waving a hand to encompass the pasture, where the alpacas are daintily nibbling the scrub; the store, guarded by the cats Knit and Purl; and the low-slung house, with Charlie, their Pyrenean mountain dog,

maintaining a vigil on the doorstep, she says: "Then this just kind of happened all at once. It was like the stars aligned when we needed them to."

Connie and Thomas took many drives out of Portland, where they'd raised their kids, to check out property in the Hood River Valley area. They found the ranch, which was, recalls Connie, "kind of junky." Around the same time, they met a nearby alpaca rancher who explained to them how the animals could help bring in money, via their highly-prized and super-soft wool, not to mention tax benefits. Connie was sold, but Thomas took a little more persuading. "I grew up on a farm

ABOVE RIGHT
The lower barn

BELOW RIGHT
Foothills Yarn and Fiber store

OPPOSITE
Thomas and Connie Betts with their herd

and I've always loved animals," she says. "But Thomas was a city guy. His mom didn't even let him have a dog." A year working as manager on a neighboring alpaca ranch converted Thomas; now he speaks about his charges with the zeal of the new convert.

One of the first things the Bettses discovered about alpacas was their not-insignificant cost: Their average price is around $10,000, but this can rise to $100,000 and above, depending on breeding history, sex and color. They started the business with four pregnant alpacas — Jasmine, Mamani, Zamora and Snow White — and though, as Connie says, "you finance them as you would a car, making a down payment and further installments while they're reproducing," they installed the yarn shop as a key element of the business. The Bettses offer visitors spinning-wheel demonstrations, and sell packets of handspun yarn (each labeled with a picture of the alpaca that it came from), as well as hats and scarves. (One of the herd's fleeces, from Snow White's son Royal Dutch, recently won a prestigious award at the national alpaca conference; the cup is proudly displayed in-store.) On weekends, she says, they have between 15 and 20 cars parked in their drive; on their busiest-ever day, she counted 28. This year, they'll be open seven days a week for the first time, a testament to the success of the Hood River County Fruit Loop, a coalition of local farms, orchards and wineries that has produced a 35 mile "route map," encouraging visitors to stop by various attractions, including Cascade Alpacas.

This small-scale local co-operation chimes with Connie's vision of her business as "a green, whole-cycle, full-circle kind of operation. Alpacas are remarkably low-maintenance for livestock — all you have to do is feed them, shear them, let them out to pasture and clean out the barn — and I just feel so good about the product we're selling and the fact that it was all produced here." That's why, despite healthy revenues of $100,000 last year, she's not interested in standard models of growing the business. "We're not interested in having a concession in every airport," she says. "I don't want the stress of having employees or management or responsibility. I mean, some days we don't have time to go to the bathroom, but I don't mind — this is fun for me."

Would she advise imminent retirees in the Bettses' position to take a similar leap in the dark? "We were lucky," she says. "We had the flexibility to gradually ease into this and wind down our other jobs. But I think our success shows that an entrepreneur doesn't necessarily have to have youth on their side." As she speaks, Cassandra, their youngest and friendliest alpaca, comes up for a nuzzle. "And I'd have missed out on all this," she says, giving Cassandra a squeeze. "So I say if you have a passion about something, then go for it, whatever your age."

Name:	JINSOO TERRY
Company:	ADVANCED GLOBAL CONNECTIONS
Industry:	CONSULTING
Location:	SAN FRANCISCO, CA

"If Jinsoo can do it, you can do it too." That's the motto — and mantra — of quite possibly the most motivated 50-year-old Korean entrepreneur you'll ever meet. In fact, so motivated is Jinsoo Terry that she's spreading her message to other immigrants, business leaders and, if she has her way, the entire world. "I'm all about overcoming weakness and setbacks, and helping people unlock their potential," she says.

Terry founded her company, Advanced Global Connections (AGC), in 2004, with the aim of training immigrants in communication skills and leadership. She runs two-week training seminars for Asian-born executives working for foreign Fortune 500 companies to help them get the hang of American business etiquette, and, she says, "to remove their fear and exploit their strengths." She employs the same techniques to help American companies motivate — that word again — their foreign-born workforce's often untapped leadership and communication skills. She's a hot ticket on the motivational-speaker circuit, and is a regular columnist in the *Korea Times*, the largest English-language Korean newspaper, in which she elaborates on her philosophy that business should be "F.U.N." — the acronym she coined for "Fun, Unconventional and Nurturing."

Executives who take her courses have to be prepared to wear socks on their heads or attend meetings on cable cars in her native San Francisco, while AGC board meetings are routinely accessorized with plastic-bird-pens and party hats. "Humor is incredibly important in removing mental blocks," she says. "You shouldn't be afraid to look ridiculous." Such daring initiatives in breaking down management/workforce barriers have already won Terry the U.S. Chamber of Commerce's Minority Business Advocate of the Year award.

Terry's path to success was fittingly unconventional. She blazed a trail in Korea by pursuing a career in engineering — still a male preserve — and, at 30, came to the U.S. with her husband, very little English and even less money: $100. She worked hard in such various industries as textiles and medical-equipment

OPPOSITE
*Jinsoo Terry, C.E.O.
of Advanced Global
Connections*

ABOVE RIGHT
*Terry demonstrates
her F.U.N.
motivational technique*

RIGHT
Terry on the move

manufacturing, but failed to make headway thanks to her poor communication skills. "It was the classic immigrant story," she says. "I thought success would come very easily, but people couldn't understand me and I couldn't make any connections." After 10 years, she was fired — and resolved to reinvent herself.

She founded her own public speaking forum, the Rhinoceros Business Club, taking inspiration from that animal's thick skin and relentless onward charge. "I started to exchange ideas with business leaders and to mentor young people who felt trapped in the same way that I did," she says. "I started to realize that communication was the key thing if you weren't going to be left behind in a multicultural business world. They heard about my activities in Korea, and asked me to submit ideas on how I would train their executives. That's how AGC was born; it all kind of happened by accident."

It seems to be a winning formula — she now employs nearly 30 people and is expecting revenues close to $2 million this year, she says — and she's founded a new company, Jinsoo Terry Enterprises, to launch what she calls "the Jinsoo brand" beyond the business community.

There's talk of a line of self-help comics featuring a character called Palbot (a friendly robot who teaches you the mores of your adopted country) and an autobiography called *Why Not Melt?* A CD, *The Jinsoo Revolution*, is in the works (on which she reaches out to youth, via some exuberant rapping), and she says that her ultimate ambition would be to host a TV business talk show. "I used to say I was a cultural counselor," she says with her ever-present grin. "Now I see myself as more of an entertainer. I love owning my own business because I can constantly challenge myself. I want to use my position to help people understand other cultures and become leaders, whatever their field."

ABOVE
Multi-tasking Terry irons out her schedule while at lunch

OPPOSITE
Terry with her comic-book creator, Caleb Hong

Name:	DANIEL LEADER
Company:	BREAD ALONE
Industry:	FOOD & BEVERAGE
Location:	BOICEVILLE, NY

It's a bitterly cold, clear winter's day in the Catskill Mountains of upstate New York, but inside Bread Alone, a bakery-café in the tiny town of Boiceville, the atmosphere is all alluring warmth. The funky interior — tables bedecked with bouquets of spring flowers and orange walls hung with vintage photos of Bob Dylan (this is Woodstock country, after all) — has something to do with it. But, principally, it's the smells — of freshly baked loaves and rolls of olive and onion focaccia or San Francisco sourdough — that evoke the spirit of hearth and home. There couldn't be a better ad for what Bread Alone's founder, Daniel Leader, calls "the soulful and sensual qualities" of bread. "There is no one who doesn't like the sight or smell of it coming out of the ovens," says Leader. "It evokes warm, gratifying feelings, and it has a universal appeal."

Wiry, buzz-cut and impassioned, Leader is holding court in the middle of the expansive

bakery that opens out behind the café. Outside are the vans that will ship Leader's 20-plus lines of Bread Alone organic loaves to his three other cafés in New York State, as well as his 150 East Coast wholesale outlets, including New York City's farmers' markets, and upscale chains such as Whole Foods Market and Dean & DeLuca. "My first principle with this place?" he asks, as roll-laden trolleys clatter past him. "To make traditional European-style artisanal bread in wood-fired brick ovens. No more, no less."

One might gather that the 52-year-old Leader is an evangelist for dough. But it wasn't always so. Twenty-five years ago, he was a graduate of the prestigious Culinary Institute of America, working as a chef in the kitchens of several exclusive Manhattan restaurants. "I spent nine years doing that," he says, shaking his head. "But they were old-school French restaurants that closed every August. And when they did, I'd go back to France with the chefs and explore the artisanal food culture of Europe. I was never really into the fancy or macho or entertainment sides of food preparation that you get in the prestige kitchens. So when these guys in France started introducing me to their favorite little bakeries, places that had been handed down from fathers or uncles, where recipes had been handed down for generations, it really struck a chord with me. And the bread was so delicious, of course. One of them said, 'Dan, I bet bread like this is really popular in the U.S.' And I thought, 'It isn't right now — but it could be.'"

Back home, Leader decided to moonlight at a bakery in Little Italy from 11 p.m., when his restaurant shifts ended, to 3 a.m. This dedication, coupled with the recipes he'd been collecting from 50 bakeries in

OPPOSITE
Dan Leader, master baker and founder of Bread Alone

LEFT
Preparing a batch of loaves

six countries, gave him the grounding he needed. "I wasn't sure if there'd be an audience for the products I wanted to create. And I had no business plan. I now teach bakery-management classes at baking schools, and I always tell the students never to start a business the way I did." He shakes his head. "It was fun from a romantic point of view, but you learn things the hard way."

Luckily, Leader's missionary zeal happened to coincide with the explosive interest in all things foodie that, two decades on, has produced the Food Network, celebrity chefs and the kind of intense interest in food preparation and provenance that Bread Alone, with its small-scale European artisanal tradition, can turn to account. It ticks all the soul-food boxes: Everything made by hand and on the premises? Check — they get through around 100,000 pounds of flour a month. All-organic ingredients? Check — it's actually the only certified-organic artisanal bakery in the New York metropolitan area.

When Leader started Bread Alone he offered five types of bread; now, he says cheerfully, "I don't even know how many we do." With the growth of his business, he's had to face the major question that entrepreneurs in his position usually face: how to build on what they have while staying true to what they are. But to Leader, small-ish really is beautiful. "I have a friend who says to me that if you own a small business in America, you're doing something that's really against the grain," he says, grinning. "The conventional expansion model would be for us to get snapped up by a big conglomerate and have mass-produced frozen Bread Alone par-baked breads in every supermarket in the country. But we don't want to play that game. We're comfortable and

rooted here, and we don't want to compromise our hand-crafted, hand-baked ethos. There's a lot of value in being an independent, privately-held business, rather than asking how fast we can grow or how quickly we can sell out." He smiles sheepishly.

But he also believes there's a moral dimension to the promotion of good nutrition, something he's putting into effect a long way from the flour-dusted floors of Boiceville. The South African Whole Grain Bread Project is a scheme conceived by Leader and some Woodstock partners to establish community-based micro-bakeries in South Africa. "We want to produce fortified bread to help improve the nutrition of malnourished people there, particularly those living with H.I.V. and AIDS," he says. Leader is hoping to follow up with job-training and teaching programs, and is also in discussions with the African Center for the Constructive Resolution of Disputes (ACCORD) about the idea of using the bakeries as community-building projects for conflict resolution. "I'm trying to use the skills I've honed in my bakery and as an entrepreneur in a new way and new direction to do something good in the world," he says.

"I suppose I'd have to call myself a businessman," concedes Leader, as the flour trucks roll in and a batch of peasant loaves are loaded onto trays. "I have to be responsible for retirement plans and health insurance and all those things. That's fine — small businesses are the engines of growth in many societies and I love the challenges that running my own business brings. But I see this as more than just a business." He sniffs as the peasant loaves are wheeled past; the aroma is heady and his smile is verging on the beatific. "I see it as a kind of calling."

ABOVE
A customer at the Woodstock café

OPPOSITE
Aiyana Berman-Waner (left) and Caitlyn Ball at the Woodstock café

CAFÉ SPECIALTIES

Tossed House Salad Fresh Seasonal Greens with our
    Crunchy Croutons & Balsamic Dressing $3.25
    with Grilled Chicken or Tofu $5.25
Caesar Salad Crisp Romaine Leaves freshly dressed with our
    Creamy Caesar, topped with Crunchy Croutons $4.95
    with Grilled Chicken or Tofu $6.95
Quiche of the Day served with Tossed House Salad $5.95

SOUP

Daily Selections $4.50
    served with Fresh Daily Bread Selection

SALADS
Celebrate the seasons with our delicious daily selections

Israeli Cous Cous Salad with Currants & Capers

Pesto Chicken Salad

Sesame Noodles

Taxes not included

ARTISAN BREADS

Baguette $2.25
Demi Baguette $1.25
Challah $4.50
Focaccia Herb Loaf $3.75
Focaccia Olive & Onion Loaf $4.25
Organic Mixed Grain $3.75
Organic Whole Wheat Sourdough (Miche) $3.75
Organic French Sourdough (Levain) $3.75
Peasant Bread $3.75
Raisin Nut Bread $4.75
Organic San Francisco Sourdough $3.75
Organic Sour Rye $3.75
Semolina Sesame $3.75
Organic Spelt Bread $4.50
Whole Grain Health Bread Organic Ingredients $4.50
Brioche $5.50

Ask us about our seasonal specials

SPECIALTY CAKES

Are our specialty!
Our Pastry Department can accommodate any request.
Some examples of our fine Specialization and Wedding Cakes
can be found on our website.
www.breada...

Name:	DR. LYNN McMAHAN
Company:	SOUTHERN EYE CENTER
Industry:	MEDICAL
Location:	HATTIESBURG, MS

There's a family feel to the Southern Eye Center (motto: "Your eyes are everything"), an ophthalmology clinic in the small town of Hattiesburg, Mississippi. Patients greet staff in the cheery waiting rooms like old friends ("Are you still seein' that policeman, darlin'?"); grateful testimonials are displayed on a board ("Thank you for saving my eyes you were cool," from Ashley, aged seven). The genial character of the place is personified in its owner, Dr. Lynn McMahan, 60. His scrubs are adorned with blue hearts or green frogs; he hums tunes or sings "Amazing Grace" during operations — with particular emphasis on the line "was blind, but now I see." "What we aim to do here is take the dread out of surgery," he says in his laconic southern drawl. "In fact, we prefer the term 'procedure.' There's no E.R. drama and blood and people shouting; you just walk in, lay down, get some drops put in, and 10 minutes later you're on your way home to cook supper." He smiles. "It's pretty fulfilling work."

McMahan founded the Center in his hometown some 30 years ago in an old fried-chicken store: "Just me and a technician," he says. "There was a need for eye specialists; the nearest were about 100 miles away. I learned the rudiments of laser surgery and brought the first laser treatments to this area." Now he and six partners, all experts in their field — McMahan on cataracts, Francis Soans on glaucoma, C. Byron Smith on corneas, etc. — operate from a custom-built clinic with a staff of 85; they perform around 6,000 operations a year on patients from all over the Gulf Coast. "I was surprised at the initial growth, but I've come to

expect it," says McMahan. "With medicine, it seems the market is never saturated."

But there's more to McMahan's practice than the rigors of the marketplace. He might enjoy all the trappings of the successful surgeon — he's lectured abroad on his techniques, met Nelson Mandela and the first President Bush and commutes in his helicopter when the mood takes him — but he sees a moral dimension to his work. "We have a rule here that we never turn anybody away," he says. "In my first year of practice, I had a lady come here with glaucoma. Several years later, she came back and she was blind. I said, 'Why didn't we see you sooner?' She said she had no insurance and couldn't afford it. If I'd seen her in time, I could have saved her sight. And I never wanted that on my conscience again." He shakes his head. "Ever."

To that end, the Center holds twice-yearly Gift Of Sight days, where eye exams and "procedures" are provided free for the poor and homeless, "people who fall through the healthcare cracks, for whatever reason, and who really need us," according to McMahan. A similar generosity of spirit prevailed after

OPPOSITE
Dr. Lynn McMahan

RIGHT
Kim Domingue, ambulatory surgery center clerk

Hurricane Katrina: The Center (which, two years on, is still missing part of its roof that was blown off by the storm) loaded up two vans with equipment and drove through the devastated area in the perilous days after the storm hit. "We were able to treat some people in the shelters whose eyes had been damaged by the flying debris," says McMahan. "Then we ran a bus down there to bring people back to the Center who needed help. Their records had been lost, they had no cards, wallets, nothing. So we just told them to walk on in and we did what we could to help."

The Center's charitable activities mean that it is the only clinic ever to be awarded the state governor's GIVE award for excellence in volunteerism; the Gift of Sight program also won *USA Today*'s National Make a Difference Day Award in 2002. For McMahan, the flexibility inherent in running a small business is key to his, well, vision. "We've been able to pioneer and test out new techniques in a way that larger establishments wouldn't have been able to," he says. "And we've also been able to maintain the personal touch with our employees and patients."

That's why, despite the fact that he's approaching retirement age, you'd have to look at McMahan for a long time before the word "jaded" ever sprang to mind. "I'm excited almost every day that I go to work," he says. "The beauty of eye surgery is that the results are almost instantaneous and you have very few failures. We don't think of our patients as cash-flow; in fact, I sometimes find it hard to think of us as a 'business' in the traditional sense. Where else can you take a blind person at 8 a.m. and have them out the door by nine with their vision back and loving you for the rest of your life? I get hugs, cards, and thank-you notes. And I get paid for it too!"

OPPOSITE
Dr. McMahan with one of his patients

ABOVE RIGHT
Eye examination using a phoropter

RIGHT
The exterior of the Southern Eye Center

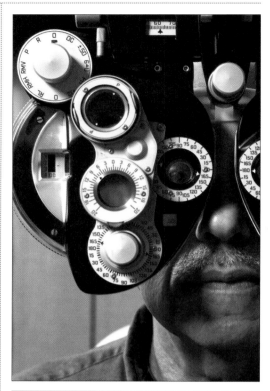

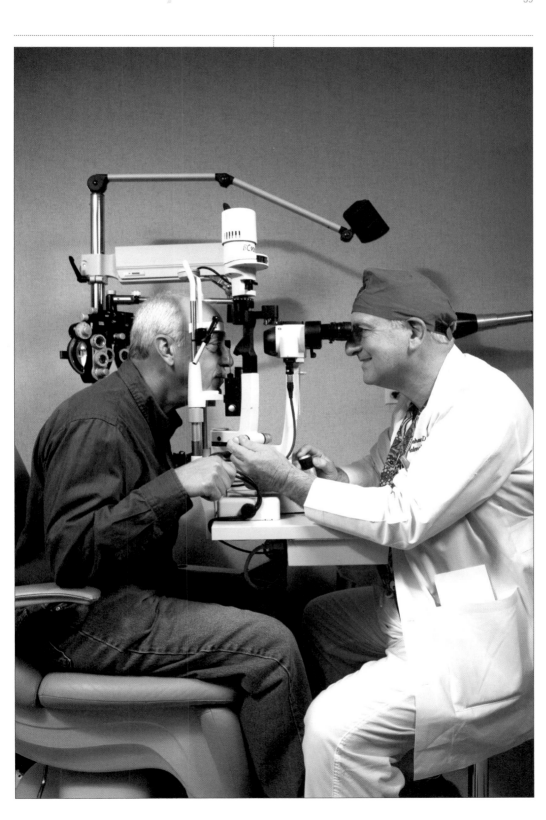

FINANCIAL ADVICE

FROM INVESTMENT TO FINANCING, HERE IS SOME SOUND FISCAL GUIDANCE AND VALUABLE POINTERS FROM OUR CASH FLOW, CREDIT AND SALES EXPERTS

1. BORROW BETTER: HOW TO GET A LOAN AND KEEP IT

Loans are big business for small business owners. Even applying for a simple credit facility can mean risking a lot. But a well-prepared borrower can negotiate from a position of strength, saving thousands of dollars. Before going out with your hat in your hand, remember these six keys to borrowing success:

— *Make it personal*

Long before you need a loan, you need a personal relationship with the lender. Loans are about trust, and trust starts with familiarity. Invite a banker to your place of business; impress them with product samples, maybe even take them out to lunch. A good relationship with a banker (or two) can benefit your business in other ways. Take advantage of their experience and contacts by asking for their help on non-banking issues. Ask a banker to join a formal board of business advisors and you may learn more about your own business as well as theirs.

— *Know the numbers*

Every business loan has terms and covenants that may require you to meet or maintain certain operating parameters. Those restrictions could mandate certain profits, cash flows, or balance sheet ratios. Be prepared by reading up on these crucial business metrics in a book such as *Annual Statement Studies*, published by the Risk Management Association, or R.M.A. for short.

The R.M.A. guide includes common financial ratios and composite financial statements culled from more than 360 industries. You can get a glimpse into the mind of a banker by picking up a copy at your local bookstore, library or bank. Alternatively, download just the pages you need for your industry at *rmahq.org*. Benchmark ratios from the R.M.A. statements are likely to become your targets to qualify for, or to maintain, commercial credit.

— *Sweeten the deal*

What banks want even more than profitable loans are customers who use savings and checking accounts and fee-generating services. If a loan request is your first and only contact with a bank, be prepared for a polite refusal. Instead, offer your bank a reward for structuring an attractive loan — shift your business checking accounts, payroll accounts and wire transfers to the lender. If your business accounts are slim, consider moving your personal mortgage or retirement savings. The more benefit for the bank you can offer, the more the bank will reward you with favorable rates and terms.

— *Plan not to fail*

If you want to win a banker's trust, show that you know all the ways your business could potentially fail. Write down 10 challenges your business faces — and the ways in which you would overcome those challenges. A list of potential pitfalls will show that you are prepared for success, and will also pre-empt many questions from the loan review committee that could slow approval.

Don't ignore the biggest risk to your business: key-person risk. If you or your business partners are incapacitated (or die) tomorrow, could you repay the loan? Key-person risk is present in every business and can best be addressed by investing in a substantial life-insurance policy. It's not unusual for banks to require insurance valued at twice the loan balance. It's morbid, and may be expensive, but it shows that you are helping the bank reduce its exposure to risk.

— *Budget pessimistically*

A thorough business plan with clear projections is vital to getting a loan approved. But projections that are too optimistic will get you into trouble. Remember that nothing ever goes as planned, so a pessimistic budget is the best kind. You will sleep better at night knowing that you have a little padding built into your numbers, and the bank will be impressed when you come in under budget.

— *Stay alert*

When you've finally closed a loan and think you can relax, think again. Loan covenants may change every month or quarter, and the bank may review your credit-worthiness periodically, too. Keep a clear eye on the terms and your ability to stay within the defined parameters. Equally important, keep building your relationship with the banker — no bank is immune from shifts in policy or priority, so be sure that your relationship is one that they value.

If you can put all the pieces together — a solid relationship, a convincing business plan,

risk management, and lots of upside for the bank — you'll be ready to negotiate a generous loan package. Remember: For a well-prepared borrower, everything is negotiable.

2. SHOULD YOU BORROW OR SELL?

There are as many different ways to finance a business as there are entrepreneurs. But in the end, there are only two kinds of money: debt, which must be paid back; and equity, which represents ownership of the business. These days, smart financiers are blurring the lines between debt and equity with convertible notes, convertible stock and so-called mezzanine financing, which is a blend of both stock and loans.

Many entrepreneurs are tempted by equity investments — not least because it can be attractive to share the risk with an investor. The downside is that equity is usually the most expensive form of finance. Since they are taking risks alongside you, lenders will expect the rate of return to be high enough to make it worth

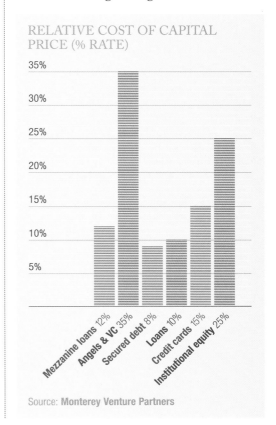

RELATIVE COST OF CAPITAL PRICE (% RATE)

Mezzanine loans 12% · Angels & VC 35% · Secured debt 8% · Loans 10% · Credit cards 15% · Institutional equity 25%

Source: **Monterey Venture Partners**

their while. While giving up a percentage of the company can be more expensive, it is still worth considering as it may provide a stable alternative to balance sheet liabilities.

Business owners love to dream that a large venture capital firm will step in with financial backing, but that's rarely how it works out. Fortunately, alternative sources of cash abound if you know where to look.

— *Do-it-yourself*
Nothing shows how serious you are about succeeding like investing your life savings into your company's growth. But choose carefully to minimize personal risk and maximize cash flow. Before taking a second mortgage on your home, look first at your life insurance policies and 401(k) plans. Ask your financial advisor if you can simply withdraw part of the death benefit, or, alternatively, take a loan against the cash value of a policy.

Many policies will allow you to pay back the principal at a flexible rate that suits your business cash needs. As a bonus, the interest may be a deductible expense for the business, and tax-deferred income for the individual. Paying yourself back can put extra money into your personal savings, plus create a higher cash balance for the next time a cash need arises.

Finally, don't forget your investments in public stocks. Traditional stockbrokerage margin accounts can free up cash quickly without liquidating your holdings, giving you a crucial tax advantage. Check with local banks first. Interest rates may be better at a lender than at your brokerage firm where the securities are held. Scout around for best rates.

— *Turn to a private equity group*
Huge private equity groups, or P.E.G.'s, have been providing liquidity for medium and large companies for decades. These days, more and more boutique or "micro P.E.G.'s" are opening their doors, and their checkbooks, to small businesses. While small business owners should carefully consider the downside of equity investments, small P.E.G.'s can offer certain advantages. Sometimes also called pledge funds, these micro funds may manage just a few million dollars, typically gleaned from the personal wealth of one or more successful entrepreneurs. Their dual mission — to buy a substantial interest in high-potential companies and lend a helping hand to the business — is a win-win formula.

KNOW THE LINGO: A GLOSSARY OF LOAN & INVESTOR TERMINOLOGY

Archangel — A respected leader in the private investor community, often an ultra-high-net-worth individual who can influence other angel investors to make an investment.

Capacity — Ability to repay a loan. Capacity compares a company's cash flow to the monthly minimum loan payment due.

Convertible debt — A loan that can be converted to stock, either by election or automatically upon reaching certain business milestones.

Convertible stock — Stock that can be converted to debt, usually at the sole discretion of the investor.

Dilution — The loss of ownership (as a percentage), which naturally results from selling company stock to new investors.

Down round — An equity investment (stock purchase) at a price lower than previous investors paid. Down rounds can cause extreme dilution to prior shareholders.

Mezzanine financing — A finance package made up of an unsecured loan combined with a grant of warrants. A mixture of debt and equity.

Participating preferred — A class of investor stock that, in case of any sale or liquidation, requires the company to pay back the initial investment before any other distributions, and also entitles the holder to participate in capital gains along with common shareholders.

Private equity group — Any organized fund or institutional investor that specializes in purchasing, and sometimes managing, private companies.

Another advantage to working with a P.E.G. is that you can put some of the investment in your pocket while the rest stays in the business for growth.

— *Go corporate*

If rapid growth is creating a cash emergency, traditional bankers, who are generally looking for "slow and steady," may not be able to help. That's where a commercial finance company can step in. Finance companies have fewer legal prohibitions than banks, but they still look for one of two things — hard assets to use as collateral or enough cash flow to comfortably make debt payments. If you have the collateral, look for "senior" or "asset-based" loans.

If you can afford to pay back the loan from cash flow, but don't have hard assets, ask about unsecured, mezzanine or subordinated loans. Subordinated and unsecured credit is widely available to businesses with solid operating profits, sometimes at two or three times the annual cash flow.

Credit card companies can provide unsecured lines of credit up to $100,000. The rates for unsecured loans depend on your credit score and are usually around the same as a credit card.

Stockbrokerage margin account — Investment account which allows you to purchase securities with funds borrowed from a broker at a specified interest rate.

Term sheet — A simple, plain-English memo which outlines the parameters of an investment or loan prior to the formal contract. Term sheets are the basis for negotiation between investor and business owner.

Valuation — The dollar value of 100% of the company stock. If an investor buys 25% of the stock for $10,000, then the valuation of the business is $40,000.

Warrants — The right to purchase stock in the future at a predetermined price (called the strike price). Similar to options of a public company, warrants are commonly used to reward early investors, consultants or lenders.

— *Raising money from angel investors*

There are many benefits to owning 100 per cent of the business you are building, but if you'd rather not go it alone, there's never been a better time to look for a wealthy partner. According to research done by the University of New Hampshire, during just the first half of 2006, more than 130,000 high-net-worth individuals — or "angel investors" — made investments in private companies, putting almost $13 billion into private companies. Unlike venture capital firms, which tend to invest exclusively in technology hotbeds, angel investors can be found in every state and city.

Since wealthy investors tend to stay out of the spotlight, finding an angel investor takes careful networking. Getting an introduction through a trusted lawyer, C.P.A. or business leader is often the best way to start negotiations with an angel. Somewhat surprisingly, however, more and more angels are banding together in clubs or investing en masse as an angel fund, making them much easier to find. The Angel Capital Education Foundation provides a list of more than 200 such groups at *angelcapitaleducation.org*.

If you decide to pursue an investment from a local angel investor or angel group, remember that it is incumbent upon you to provide full disclosure about your business — and you should expect the same in return. Learn all you can about the other investments your angel has made. Interview other entrepreneurs who have worked with him or her. Don't let the excitement of the deal cloud your judgment.

When you've found the right investor and are close to agreeing on terms, it's time to start the paperwork. Be sure to retain experienced legal counsel to prepare a private placement memorandum (P.P.M.) and stock subscription agreement. Without proper documentation, the investment can be rescinded, leaving you on the hook for a refund.

Even the best-intentioned partner may turn from helper to hindrance. If the investor wants to micro-manage your business, or worse, decides that you are mismanaging his money, beware. Too many entrepreneurs have landed in court thanks to a disgruntled partner. Usually, of course, angel investors live up to their name. Many want only to invest in growing companies and provide a small amount of help when they can.

Continues on page 46

GO WITH THE FLOW

THESE CASH MANAGEMENT STRATEGIES CAN PAY OFF HANDSOMELY IN THE LONG RUN

When you think of what makes a business healthy, you probably focus on measures like profit, sales growth or customer loyalty. But you can have all of those things and still go out of business if you don't have the one thing that all companies need: cash. It takes cash to pay employees, to pay the rent and to keep the doors open and the lights on.

Because having cash available when you need it is so critical, knowing how to measure, monitor and manage the cash that flows in and out of your business is a vital skill. Here, we have put together the five golden rules in order to make cash flow work for you instead of against you:

— KNOW HOW TO MEASURE IT

Cash flow issues will not be obvious from even the most careful review of a company's income statement. Cash, and how your company is using it, can only be seen on the balance sheet and cash flow statements. Sales, expenses and profits are important, of course, but an income statement represents only a moment in time.

A cash flow statement, on the other hand, shows the movement of money in and out of the business over a period of time. Other tools for understanding cash flow include some simple balance sheet calculations, such as the number of days it takes to turn inventory, and how long it takes for cash to cycle through your business.

If tracking these items sounds daunting, make time to speak with a savvy advisor, your C.P.A. or a finance consultant.

— KNOW THE CAUSES OF CASH FLOW PROBLEMS

Cash flow problems can come from either end of the business cycle — spending or receiving. Growth opportunities necessitate investment in inventory and infrastructure, which can use too much precious cash. On the other hand, if your customers are not paying you quickly enough, your company will not create enough cash. Of course, you might also run low on cash simply because sales have slumped.

Understanding these fundamental causes of cash flow can help you head off problems before they start. If you know that you are facing rapid growth, declining sales or long collection cycles, consider yourself forewarned and forearmed.

Name:	RAYMOND JOABAR
Job Title:	SENIOR VICE PRESIDENT AND GENERAL MANAGER OF LENDING AND NETWORK DEVELOPMENT
Joined:	1992
Responsibility:	LEADS THE CREDIT CARD PORTFOLIO AND MANAGES LINE-OF-CREDIT PRODUCTS

— BUILD STRATEGIES THAT CAN MAXIMIZE CASH FLOW

To prevent cash shortages, the best defense is a good offense, so get serious about minimizing fixed expenses. A company should be big enough to cover only its most predictable, recurring needs. Find creative ways to handle peaks in demand without hiring additional staff; outsourcing and finding interns are good strategies for "right-sizing" and minimizing cash needs.

Consider non-cash ways to make purchases. Credit card rewards programs and frequent flier points can be effective cash substitutes, as can bartering.

Finally, set clear payment terms and expectations with your customers. Consider discounts for prepayment and penalties for late payment. Knowing when you can expect payment is half the battle, but don't neglect good follow-up and collections.

— PREPARE FOR THE WORST

When cash is tight, you need tools at hand to solve the problem fast. Get a jump on the problem by lining up several sources of financing in advance. Be sure to match the sources and uses appropriately. Use short-term financing options such as lines of credit, short-term loans or credit cards for short-term cash needs, and long-term or secured loans only for the purchase of long-term investments.

— GROW SMART

Consistent growth is the best way to smooth out bumps in cash flow. When opportunities for growth present themselves, plan carefully. Make a conscious decision about how much you have to spend to meet the opportunity and how long it will be before you will be able to pay it back.

Every investment, whether in inventory, people or equipment, should have a clear return. Make sure each earns a profit, but also look at how long it will take to collect them.

Likewise, if you look at each customer as an investment with a scheduled return, you'll not only improve cash flow, but profitability, too. Allocate costs to each customer by isolating and assigning each cost in the business to a job. Don't use one job to fund another; make sure each stands on its own merits. When each job is profitable, and profits are collected on time, cash flow problems will begin to diminish.

3.   MANAGING YOUR FINANCES

As with any other aspect of your business, choose your tools carefully for the long-term management of your finances. Of course, credit and deposit accounts in the name of your business will help build the company's credit rating — and likewise prevent a problem at the company from affecting your personal credit.

If monthly expenses tend to be up one month and down the next, a credit card with a revolving balance feature can help you manage cash flow and deal with the fluctuations. On the other hand, a charge card is good if you know you can pay it in full at the end of every month and just use it as a tool to manage expenses within the payment time frame. With no pre-set spending feature it gives you the flexibility to manage unpredictable expenses such as entertainment and travel. In either case, you should look for the other benefits you'll use most, including insurance, reward points, and member discounts at your most often-used business vendors.

Savings and checking accounts should always be selected for best fit and kept separate. Interest-bearing accounts, or sweep accounts that move money into high-interest opportunities overnight, are helpful if you keep a large average balance. Overdraft protection might be more important if your balance tends to be low.

Consider whether the accounts — and the institutions behind them — will make your life easier or harder. The best accounts will link to each other, download into your accounting software and have 24-hour customer service with web access. Don't settle for less. Having the right accounts, with the right benefits, at the right institutions, can make the difference between running back and forth to the bank and running your business.

Finally, remember too that the tax man likes to see exactly how you've spent your money. Keep business and personal accounts separate. Hang on to all your receipts, or at least be sure your accounts provide good reporting, with quarterly- and annual-statement summaries. Even the most complicated income statement, expense report or tax return will be a little easier with good reports.

— *Start smart*

Starting a new business is exciting — but it can also be financially dangerous. Before you take the plunge, have adequate insurance coverage for worst-case scenarios. That means life and health insurance for you and your family, in case anything goes wrong. It also means long-term disability insurance, life policies on key employees or partners and adequate liability insurance for the business. Insure yourself by holding back some reserves, too. There's no reason to put every penny of your savings into a brand-new business. Always keep reserves for unexpected problems, market slowdowns and to finance growth.

THE IDEAL SMALL BUSINESS PORTFOLIO

30% STOCKS & BONDS

10% CASH & SAVINGS

10% INVESTMENT REAL ESTATE

10% HOME EQUITY

40% BUSINESS OWNED

Most business owners have the majority of their personal wealth tied up in their business. Diversifying into other investments is an important way to build and protect personal wealth.

Source: **Monterey Venture Partners**

— *Personal perspective — retire rich*

Most entrepreneurs love what they do and can't imagine retirement. That sentiment builds strong companies, but may not ensure a comfortable life when old age, infirmity or death severs them from their business. A rich retirement requires careful planning at every stage of life.

— *Personal considerations*

Just owning a profitable business can be enough to provide for your future if you make the most of it. This can be as simple as making sure that you set aside savings whenever possible. The discipline to live within your means, and to balance expenses with savings, can ensure a golden retirement, regardless of what happens to the business in the long-term. But saving by itself is not enough. Pay as much attention to your investments as you do to your business and you'll be on your way to a secure future. Balance your total risk by investing in lower-risk asset classes such as real estate and whole-life insurance. Both of those assets can grow significantly in value while also providing income and liquidity.

— *Make an early withdrawal*

Remember that your business was built to serve you, not the other way around. As soon as you have the opportunity, do not waste time: Boost your personal wealth by taking some of your money out of the company. That might mean selling a piece of the business to employees or partners, or simply increasing your own salary.

— *Sell high*

The sale price of your business will probably be the largest single factor affecting your wealth and your retirement. But the best price might not be available at the exact moment you want to retire. Do not wait: Remember that timing really is everything. The best time to exit your business is during strong growth and high profitability. If you are getting unsolicited offers to buy the business it may be a good time to sell.

Finally, make sure that the sale terms match perfectly with your personal financial needs. Be sure to get a qualified financial planner, C.P.A. and lawyer involved as early as possible.

4. THE BIG PICTURE: BUILD A BALANCE-SHEET-DRIVEN COMPANY

If you are focusing only on expenses and profits, you may be overlooking both the opportunities and the dangers that a deeper analysis of your balance sheet can expose:

— *Solvency*

How well are you able to meet your debt obligations in the short term? Before approving a loan, a banker will undoubtedly do an acid test on your balance sheet. Also called the Quick Ratio, this compares short-term cash to short-term debt [Cash + Accounts Receivable / Current Liabilities]. A value between 0.5 and 1.1 is considered healthy, but the higher the score the better.

If your business has inventory, also look at the Current Ratio [Current Assets / Current Liabilities]. In most industries, a value of two is considered a good minimum.

Another prime measure of solvency is the Debt-to-Equity ratio [Total Liability / Total Tangible Owner's Equity], which tells a lender how much of the business risk he's taking. Many private companies have very little equity, but when this number starts heading toward double digits, it's time to consider decreasing bank debt.

— *Efficiency*

Are you making the most of the cash in your business? The first place to look is accounts receivable. Calculate how long it takes to collect payment, called Days Outstanding [Accounts Receivable / Annual Sales x 365]. For invoice-based companies, the national average is about 45 days, but shorter is better.

When cash is tight, the next suspect is inventory — keeping too much locks up cash that may be needed in other areas. Calculate your Inventory Turnover [Annual Cost of Goods Sold / Average Value of Inventory] to see how many times your inventory turns over each year. Larger numbers are better — indicating that you are not locking up cash in excess inventory. Use the average value of your inventory and compare your result to other companies in your industry.

Continues on page 50

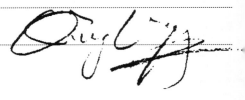

CREDIT CHECK

QING LIN GUIDES US THROUGH THE PROCESS OF SECURING CREDIT AND MEETING YOUR BUSINESS GOALS

Of all the tools in a small business owner's arsenal, perhaps none is as powerful as having good credit. The ability to access funds can be both a linchpin for growth and a temporary panacea in troubled times. Fast access to cash will help a forward-thinking entrepreneur take advantage of rapidly changing opportunities, or help a troubled business get past rough spots in the road.

But credit can be hard to find when you are most in need, so don't wait. Having good lending relationships is something that takes careful planning and attention well before the rubber meets the road. Credit card companies aim to help entrepreneurs meet their business goals by providing appropriate levels of finance. Here are the five best practices that you should consider to improve and expand your access to capital:

— BALANCE GROWTH AND RISK

Entrepreneurs are pretty good at taking risks. Not all entrepreneurs, however, are good at balancing risks with the likely reward. To build great credit, balance is key. That means planning conservatively before you use borrowed money for a project. If you consistently plan for the worst, and work for the best, you'll avoid credit problems and build a track record of success.

On the other hand, it would be counter-productive to shy away from real growth opportunities. When a golden opportunity presents itself, make the most of it. Learn how to plan both the use and repayment of funds, and then frame the opportunity in terms your lender can understand. If the opportunity is real, and you can describe it in reasonable terms, you should have no problem accessing capital.

— WHO ARE YOU DEALING WITH?

Bad credit has a tendency to be contagious. Don't let a bad customer ruin your own credit. Protect yourself from late-payers (or no-payers) by putting a reputable intermediary in the middle. Credit card companies should minimize their merchants' exposure to credit risk by always carefully approving card holders and ensuring that your receipts are cleared in a timely manner. Likewise, as a credit card holder, you ought to be protected from fraudulent transactions of any kind. And in case of any dispute about the payment, the credit card company can be a valuable third-party mediator.

Name:	QING LIN
Job Title:	CHIEF CREDIT OFFICER, OPEN
Joined:	1990
Responsibility:	LEADS CREDIT RISK PORTFOLIO AND OVERSEES EXTENSION OF CREDIT AND LINE SIZES

— KEEP BUSINESS SEPARATE

This is probably the most important tenet of building and maintaining good credit. Separating all accounts — both deposit accounts like checking and savings, and credit accounts like charge cards and loans — can seem onerous. But there is no other way to build a good credit record for your company. Separating accounts protects your personal credit score from the vagaries of business transactions. Business problems that cause missed payments are bad enough, but allowing them to impact your personal credit would be far worse.

— USE MULTIPLE CAPITAL SOURCES

Stretch your credit by using the right tool for the job. If you pay your charge card by the end of the month there is no cost of capital, so if you want a large line of money available but only pay interest on what you draw on, credit is a better option. If you have a large investment (such as land or significant equipment), then a traditional loan may be sensible. When you apply for — and properly use — multiple credit tools, you are demonstrating your ability to handle other people's money efficiently. As you demonstrate good judgment, and repayment habits, you build your creditworthiness.

— SELECT THE RIGHT PARTNER

Lenders grant credit based on "the five Cs": capacity, character, collateral, capital and conditions. In other words, they want to know if you can afford to repay a loan (capacity); are you the kind of person who is likely to repay a loan (character); what's left for the bank if you can't repay a loan (collateral); your ultimate net worth (capital); and how the current economy and your own stage in life might affect the situation (conditions).

When considering a new loan or lender, ask similar questions of them. Determine the three Cs of any lender's offer: Is it the right size loan (capacity); does it have the right repayment terms/fees (character); and does it come with the best ancillary benefits (collateral). Don't forget that even if the loan is right for you, the lender might be wrong. Find one with a solid reputation who offers you some other tools that you need to run your business.

In the end, a long-term relationship with a lender you can trust (and who learns to trust you) will pay off in better credit, and more of it.

5.   CASH FLOW FOCUS

There is a common complaint among business owners in the U.S: accounts receivable problems that are causing cash flow to stall. There are a number of ways to unlock the cash from receivables and put it to use in other parts of your business. Here's what to do if you find yourself in any of the following hypothetical situations.

—— My services business is growing fast. Income statements show a profit every month, but I never seem to have enough money to make payroll. Why is that?

It sounds like you have a collections problem. The profit showing on your income statement is not being paid by your customers quickly enough to generate real cash. Meanwhile, big expenses like payroll can't wait. It's a very common problem, particularly when you're hiring new staff to serve new clients.

Try this: Offer your clients different payment terms or methods. Allow your customers to pay by credit card, rather than by sending a check. You get your cash faster, and the customer can take as long as he needs to pay his credit card bill. If you are lucky enough to have repeat customers, offer a small discount for pre-payment. Getting paid in advance for your services will turn your cash problem upside down.

— I sell materials to manufacturers all over the country. By the time I make an invoice, mail it and get their check back in the mail, more than 50 days have passed. I'd rather have that money in the bank earning interest. What can I do?

Common accounting software packages, like QuickBooks, now offer electronic presentation and collections. QuickBooks will convert your invoices to Adobe PDF format, send them by e-mail and help you collect payment via credit card or online service. You can turn an invoice around in five minutes instead of 50 days. But before you can expect customers to pay that quickly, let them know what you expect. It helps to negotiate specific terms, including interest charges for late payers.

— My clients are Fortune 100 retailers with huge clout. When it comes to payments, they name their own terms. I love my customers, but the more they order, the harder it is for me to pay for the goods I'm shipping out. How can I balance demand with success?

Have you ever considered outsourcing your entire accounts receivable function? Hiring a finance company to approve credit, make collection calls, receive payments and make deposits can improve cash flow and save costs. Sophisticated asset-based lenders can help you focus on making money, while they focus on collecting it.

It works like this: You mail your invoices to customers as usual, but include a payment address that belongs to the lender. The lender then purchases those same accounts receivable from you, and takes responsibility for collecting the debt.

Most lenders will pay you 80 to 90 per cent of the value of the invoices in advance, with the balance paid when the invoice is collected. The fee for this service is usually simple interest on the outstanding balance (the difference between the cash paid to you, and the cash collected from your customers).

— I deal extensively with vendors and customers overseas. I might buy from China and sell in Denmark. Every day it's a different scenario. What's the best way to negotiate international currencies and make sure I get paid by companies that are thousands of miles away?

That's a tall order, but fortunately there are a number of government and private programs that can help. The U.S. government supports the Export-Import Bank, *www.exim.gov*, that makes and guarantees a variety of loans just for U.S. companies like yours. You may already use wire transfers, which are reliable, but often cost $30 or more for each transaction and may take two or more days to clear your U.S. bank. Of course, neither of those options will work in all situations, so try charge cards when you can. International charges are processed quickly and the foreign exchange rate is typically very advantageous. Apply to accept well-known international credit cards and ask your vendors if they will do the same. Having the power of a large credit company between you and your foreign partners can add another level of security in case of disputes, fraud or other unforeseen circumstances.

We're a very customer-focused organization, and strive to make our clients feel like part of our family. When they don't pay their bills, however, my skills are put to the test. How can I get people to pay their bills without jeopardizing our close working relationship?

First, be sure that the relationship is worth saving. It's good practice to "fire" your worst customers once in a while. But if you're not ready to cut them loose, designate someone else in your organization to make collections calls — preferably someone that is not otherwise in a customer-facing role. They should be polite but firm, and speak directly to each customer's accounting department. If you don't have any extra bodies around,

consider outsourcing your entire receivables function. You'll get your cash in advance, and your customers will be well-cared-for by accounting professionals.

6. HOME-COURT ADVANTAGE

Where you do business can make all the difference. Although you compete in a global marketplace, local conditions may be holding you back. Recent volatility in gasoline prices and real-estate markets has business owners scrambling to hold down costs and maintain profit margins. Business owners in some cities have a clear advantage. Take a look at the maps below and overleaf to see how two factors — office-space rent and gasoline prices — may be giving your competitors a cost advantage.

COST OF OFFICE SPACE IN DOWNTOWN LOCATIONS — $/SQ.FT. PER YEAR

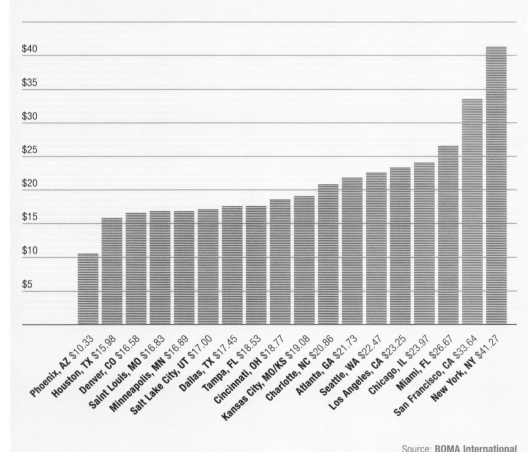

Phoenix, AZ $10.33
Houston, TX $15.98
Denver, CO $16.58
Saint Louis, MO $16.83
Minneapolis, MN $16.89
Salt Lake City, UT $17.00
Dallas, TX $17.45
Tampa, FL $18.53
Cincinnati, OH $18.77
Kansas City, MO/KS $19.08
Charlotte, NC $20.86
Atlanta, GA $21.73
Seattle, WA $22.47
Los Angeles, CA $23.25
Chicago, IL $23.97
Miami, FL $26.67
San Francisco, CA $33.64
New York, NY $41.27

Source: **BOMA International**

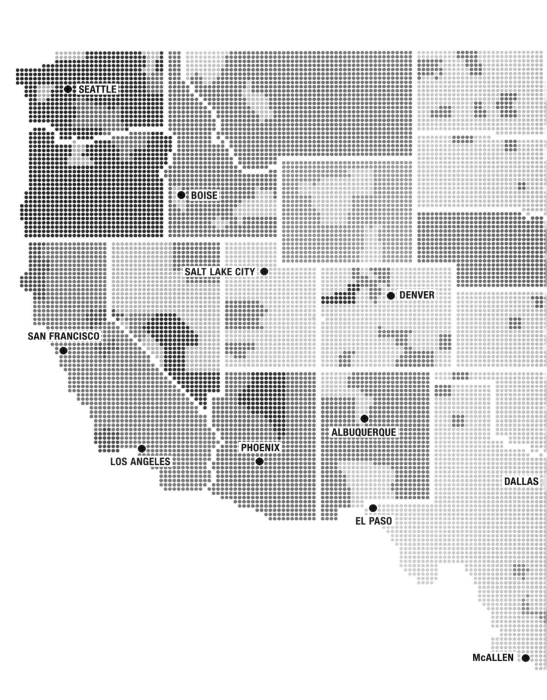

SEATTLE

BOISE

SALT LAKE CITY

DENVER

SAN FRANCISCO

ALBUQUERQUE

PHOENIX

LOS ANGELES

DALLAS

EL PASO

McALLEN

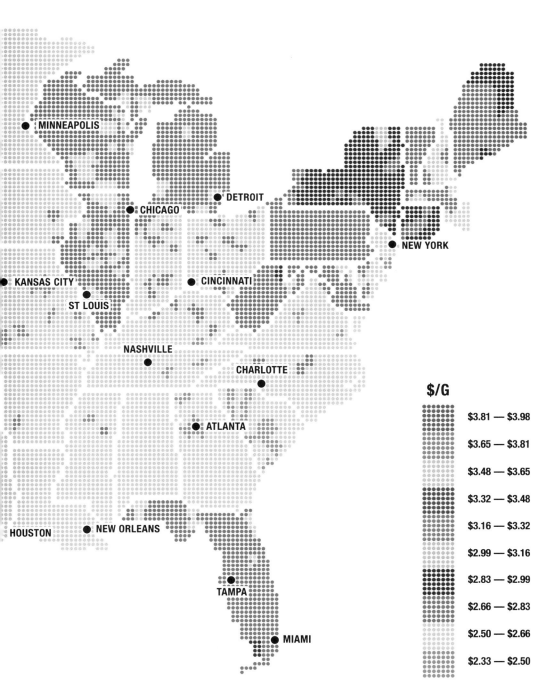

MINNEAPOLIS

DETROIT

CHICAGO

NEW YORK

KANSAS CITY

CINCINNATI

ST LOUIS

NASHVILLE

CHARLOTTE

ATLANTA

HOUSTON

NEW ORLEANS

TAMPA

MIAMI

$/G

$3.81 — $3.98

$3.65 — $3.81

$3.48 — $3.65

$3.32 — $3.48

$3.16 — $3.32

$2.99 — $3.16

$2.83 — $2.99

$2.66 — $2.83

$2.50 — $2.66

$2.33 — $2.50

THE TOP LINE

SUCCESS IN SALES TAKES MORE THAN A SMILE AND SLICK PRESENTATION — GINA SELLS US SOME SOLUTIONS

There is an old adage in business that nothing happens until somebody makes a sale. Indeed, making sales is the reason businesses exist, but exactly how to identify, acquire and keep customers can be a constant challenge. In fact, in a recent poll of small business owners' education needs, sales ranked above all other areas, including industry knowledge.

Successful selling requires pulling together what your company does best with what your prospects want most. But knowing which is which requires care and planning. To plan your own sales success, follow these five simple steps:

— KNOW YOUR U.S.P.

Why should a customer do business with you instead of a competitor? Do you provide the highest level of service, or are you the low-cost leader? Knowing what makes you unique in the market — your Unique Selling Proposition (U.S.P.) — is the first step to attracting customers.

Craft a killer U.S.P. by knowing your market inside out. Talk to prospects and customers and research the competition — understand why some customers are attracted to the competitors and why others are not. To become the market leader, describe what you

can do for the customer better than anyone else.

Be sure your U.S.P. truly captures your personal passion. Customers respond to passion, and it's one thing that makes you truly unique.

— FUNNELING THROUGH

There is a good analogy of a "purchase funnel" with three stages: awareness, consideration and application. If you understand what customers need at each stage, you can help them through the funnel more quickly. The first step is awareness — prospective customers have to learn who you are. Promotion is the key. At this stage, messages that focus on emotional benefits can be most effective. Stress emotional concepts like security, comfort, charity, integrity or prestige.

At the consideration stage, prospects begin weighing the pros and cons of making a purchase. Sales pitches that include rational, quantifiable benefits — cost savings, for example — will push them over the hump.

— SET UP LISTENING POSTS

Current customers can tell you what you're doing right and ex-customers can speak about what you're doing wrong. If you

Name:	GINA TAYLOR
Job Title:	VICE PRESIDENT OF CARD ACQUISITION
Joined:	1997
Responsibility:	LEADS CREDIT- AND CHARGE-CARD SALES TO SMALL BUSINESS OWNERS

listen carefully you'll learn what each group needs and how they make purchase decisions; information you can use to your advantage.

To get this valuable information on a budget, consider building low-cost "listening posts" on the Internet. Ask customers to take a Web-based survey or visit a chat room where they can discuss their needs. Use these forums to start an open and honest dialogue with, and between, customers. Each time you have contact with a customer, create opportunities for feedback. Make everyone in your organization responsible for creating their own listening posts. Use the feedback to guide new promotional messages and new product offerings.

— FOCUS CLEARLY
Focus can turn light into laser beams. In the same way, a focused sales effort can turn prospects into customers. Focusing sales means knowing which customers will be most receptive to your U.S.P. If you're selling high service at a premium price, it's important to get your sales message to those customers that can afford — and will appreciate — your superior service.

What do your best customers look like? Where do they work? What do they read?

When you know how your prospective customer behaves, you can better identify how to reach them. Will an ad in a magazine deliver your message better than a billboard? Effective selling is not about making impressions, it's about getting those impressions to the right target market at the right time.

— MARKET AND WALLET SHARE
Having a dominant share of the market is an admirable goal. But just as important is what's called "wallet share" — how much of what your customers buy are they buying from you? It's often easier and more profitable to sell something to an existing customer than a new one. By maximizing your sales to each customer, you can reduce the cost of sales and increase profits.

It is important to keep on looking for ways to provide complementary value to existing customers. As you provide them with increasing value, the likelihood of losing them to the competition becomes much lower. Strong companies are built on loyalty, and customer loyalty is built by continuously giving them more of what they need.

NET GAINS

"NETREPRENEURS" CUBAN COUNCIL IMPART SOME ADVICE ON HOW TO DEVELOP A WEB PRESENCE THAT WILL DRIVE SALES AND REACH NEW CUSTOMERS

A great number of small businesses are adding a Web site to their enterprise. How well they utilize the medium is another story. With word of mouth as the most tangible marketing currency, the quickest way to reach a multitude of potential customers is via their browser or inbox. Measuring the power of your Web site is relatively easy, although not necessarily indicative of target. Attracting people to your product, especially if you've honed the offering to perfection, is suddenly less time-consuming than before the Web.

However, it's no use uploading a half-hearted Web site with poor navigation and sloppy design — after all, your site is a very public brand extension, and often the first introduction you'll make to a new customer. Everything from the name to the nature of the content must be given serious consideration, because you don't want to lose anyone at the first hurdle.

And for those technophobes and proud Luddites out there, the process of creating a Web site is not the code-addled, mindbending trip that you might imagine. Simplified programs and applications for enthusiasts, in addition to a long-awaited drop in inflated Web agency fees, mean that registering, creating and uploading a Web site tailored to your needs is easier than ever. With the correct marketing strategy you are no longer limited to the U.S. market, but can spread across the Internet and make inroads in markets that were once impossible for domestic businesses to penetrate. What follows are a few suggestions that will help you make the most of your site.

1.   GET A MEMORABLE DOMAIN

Most people don't remember .org and .tv domains so go for the good old .com where possible. While most three-letter .com domains and many common words and names are already taken, there are still some creative alternatives. Since many simple noun domains such as *architects.com* are long gone, consider going with a verb, action or phrase like *buildingthefuture.com*. Keep your domain name short, simple and easy to spell. Tools like Instant Domain Search (*instantdomainsearch.com*) check for availability as you type, which makes it easier to come up with an original name. Make sure you spend the extra cash and get the peripheral domain names like .org and .net as well. As soon as your site starts gaining traffic,

domain name squatters will scoop those alternative sites up if you haven't already.

2. OUTSOURCE YOUR WEB HOSTING

Hosting your Web site on your own server can be costly and cause many headaches. There are many great hosts that have already invested capital in power failure-backup-systems, storage protection, servers and technical staff. With plans that cost about $20 per month for a shared or grid-based server or $100 per month for a dedicated one, you'll keep your overall costs down and increase service levels. Great hosts include Media Temple (*mediatemple.net*) and Tilted (*tilted.com*).

3. DESIGN FOR YOUR AUDIENCE

A Web site is as much about aesthetics as it is about information. Make sure the design not only reflects your company, but also appeals to your customers. If you hire a Web design agency for your site, make sure their style matches up with yours. Be sure to take a look at their portfolio and check references, and don't be scared to ask questions or feel confused in initial meetings; you're paying for a service and a good agency will make time to take you through the whole process. Resist the urge for flashy graphics and animation unless it's absolutely necessary — simplicity is always the best policy.

4. WATCH HOW PEOPLE USE YOUR SITE

Even if you can't have user testing done professionally, you can always do a simple round yourself. Look over the shoulder of a friend, family member or employee while they are using your site. Ask them to find a section or perform a task, such as make a purchase. Also, try to observe people from a range of demographics — this will give you a good idea of how "usable" and customer-friendly your site is. Not everyone is Web-savvy, and you risk alienating a large proportion of your target market if your site is too user-unfriendly.

5. KEEP YOUR EYE ON THE STATS

Every commercial site, no matter how aesthetically pleasing, needs to generate demonstrable results. You can constantly improve your conversion rate or click-through rate by keeping on top of your Web stats. Many Web hosts (and services such as Google

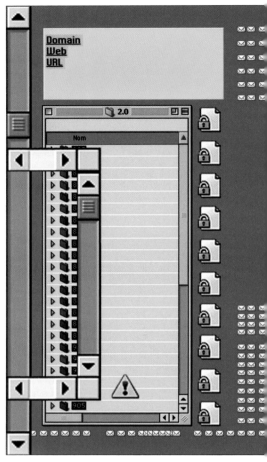

Analytics) offer real-time reports for free. Also, check *alexa.com* for Web traffic rankings for your site and those of your competitors. You can even compare your traffic with another site, be it a competitor or Google, to see how you match up. There are other solutions available as well, such as the neat online statistics application Mint (*haveamint.com*), which helps you get an idea how traffic flows on your site, and what other Web sites link to your business.

6. KEEP YOUR CONTENT FRESH

Nothing turns away a customer faster than out-of-date content or a Web site that never gets updated. But, before you throw in the towel right away, you don't need to have a full-time Web designer to do this. A content management system (C.M.S.), which could be custom-built or off-the-shelf, makes updating a Web site as easy as filling out a form and uploading a photo. It is always better to have the C.M.S. tool built

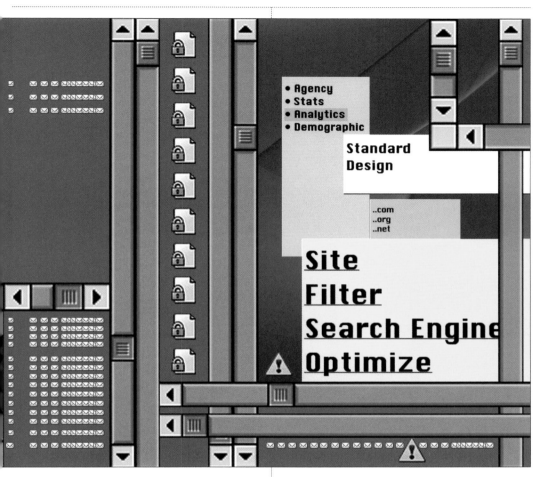

into your site, instead of trying to reverse-engineer it into an existing site. With a system like this in place you can successfully update your content without having to worry about any extra expenditure or costly man-hours.

7. OPTIMIZE YOUR SEARCH ENGINES

Search engines, like Yahoo! and Google, are usually the first place people will look for you. Make it easier for them to find you. Yahoo! and Google offer tools to let them know the site map structure of your Web site. Also, using clean U.R.L.'s like *yourdomain.com/store/widgets* instead of *yourdomain.com/store.php?id=42&categoryID= widgets* will increase your chances of getting indexed in a search engine. Finally, don't waste money on so-called Search Engine Optimization (S.E.O.) specialists. Search engines are very quick to penalize sites that

try to trick their filtering techniques, and once your site has been put on Google's blacklist, it will take forever to get off.

8. STAY AHEAD OF TECHNOLOGY

When planning and building your Web site, make sure to keep it fairly simple in order to maximize the number of potential visitors. Remember that not all people browse the Web using computers — it is increasingly normal to access the Web via cell phones, P.D.A.'s and other fast-developing technologies.

Cuban Council is a young design group that specializes in the development of creative concepts for Web and print applications. Its mission statement is "to design and develop digital solutions that are fun and usable." The team works across a diverse range of industries, and platforms and runs k10k, one of the Web's premier design portals.
www.cubancouncil.com

Marcella Shinder

BRAND VALUES

ONCE YOU'VE DEVELOPED THE BEST POSSIBLE PRODUCT, HOW DO YOU TURN YOUR OFFERING INTO A SUCCESSFUL BRAND?

What is branding? Most of us have some idea of what it is, but — through no fault of our own — few understand its essence. Over time we have built immunity to corporate jargon, and in doing so, we have discounted the significance of branding as a useful tool in developing a successful business. Branding is not simply your visual identity, the execution of logo and design; it is much more than that. Effective branding will drive growth, increase sales and assist in attracting and retaining customers.

By definition, your brand is the distinctive name identifying your product, but beyond your name it's the associations that people make when they think about you. It's the telephone manner of your employees, the efficiency of your service and the memorable nature of the overall experience. Branding is the most important element in any company's dialogue with its customer. Branding is the face, voice and personality of your business. It signifies reputation, loyalty and emotional attachment, and any enterprise that pays no heed to the importance of branding risks anonymity and isolation. Essentially, branding is the promise you make based upon your core offering.

Of course, the principal concern for any entrepreneur is developing the best product or service in their field. With excellence as standard, a business is in an enviable position to build a brand around this core offering. Your brand plays a key role in differentiating you from the competition, and helps communicate your key message to the consumer. On these pages are five easily actionable principles to which any business can subscribe; designed to assist entrepreneurs in every industry, these five brand tenets guide the small business owner by asking some fundamental questions.

— WHY AM I DIFFERENT?
There should be one thing imprinted on your consciousness, and even on your subconscious, and that's the very thing that sets your product or service apart from every other in the market: your U.S.P. (Unique Selling Proposition). And if you can communicate the "Aha" moment — that inspirational flash you had at the conception of your business which still drives you forward — to your customers, then half your work is done.

Name:	MARCELLA SHINDER
Job Title:	VICE PRESIDENT OF BRAND MARKETING AND STRATEGY
Joined:	1993
Responsibility:	OVERSEES OPEN'S BRAND MARKETING PROGRAM

— WHAT IS MY VISION?

The old adage that "Rules were made to be broken" simply doesn't apply to branding. You may add or update, but the rules you create for your own brand should stand the test of time. By building a foolproof mission statement and sticking to it you are in a better position to educate and inspire those you know and those you don't. The simpler the statement, the easier it will be to remember and convey to your customers.

— HOW DO I COMMUNICATE MY BRAND?

Once you have identified your unique offer and vision, you have to begin packaging it accordingly. It starts with a visual system (see Make Your Marque on page 62) and flows through every customer (and employee) touchpoint. Everything — from your business cards to your business garb, from the way you answer the phone to the décor of your office, from the sales materials you leave with customers and prospects to your Web presence. Every touchpoint must reflect, reinforce and reiterate your core brand identity.

— HOW DO I MAKE SURE MY BRAND IS THE RIGHT ONE?

It is important to consider how your brand is reflected at each touchpoint with a customer: from how your receptionist greets them at the door to the materials you might leave behind after a sales meeting. Ask your customers how they perceive your brand and then ask yourself whether that is the impression you are intending. If the two are not in agreement, think about ways in which you can better get the message across.

— HOW DO I STAY TRUE TO MY BRAND?

We can't all wake up every day with a smile on our face and a spring in our step, but a healthy brand demands perseverance and perspiration from everyone involved. Injecting your brand with all the energy it deserves will ensure longevity and hearty returns. To promote optimism, augment your mission statement with the top five core business values that will keep you true to your brand and post these in a place both you and your employees will see every day as a constant reminder to all.

BELOW
The original Poppy logo as seen on the door to the Nolita store

BOTTOM
Poppy's interior space welcomes customers and encourages them to browse

OPPOSITE
The Poppy storefront showcases an eclectic mix of fashion and objets d'art

MAKE YOUR MARQUE

YOUR VISUAL IDENTITY IS THE FIRST AND MOST IMPORTANT CONTACT YOU HAVE WITH THE OUTSIDE WORLD — MAKE THE MOST OF IT WITH A CONSIDERED DESIGN PROGRAM

Developing a brand identity can often seem like the preserve of big companies with large marketing budgets — and the consultants and agencies on whom they spend them. In fact, an organization of any size can and should enjoy the benefits that a good brand identity brings to business. At its simplest, a well-expressed brand can give you the same kind of advantage a well-cut suit might present at a sales meeting. Beyond that, your brand identity can be a tangible symbol of the goodwill your business earns, positively influencing your value while also providing some insulation against the difficulties that can arise from time to time in business life.

True to its origins in the marking of property, most people associate a brand with the visual sign or symbol a business uses to identify itself. Certainly one of the hallmarks of a successful brand is when a company's symbol is instantly recognizable, without the need to spell its name out in words. But to get to that point all the factors that underpin a brand, sometimes invisibly, need to be well established. If a visual identity represents the flowering of your brand, it will need the ongoing support of healthy roots, stems and leaves to feed and support it. Understanding how all this fits together for your

THIS PAGE

The Poppy team presents the current corporate identity as seen on all the point-of-sale applications, including packaging and stationery

DESIGN GLOSSARY

Brand identity — the expression of your business philosophy in all its applications that customers, staff and suppliers will see.

Logo — the graphic symbol of your organization, deployable across all media.

Logotype — the typographical treatment — font, spacing, layout — of your company name.

Palette — the selection of colors defined for use in the visual expression of your brand, the palette is referenced in Pantone or CMYK for consistent output from your print supplier.

Tagline — a phrase that appears with your logo and says the first thing you want to be associated with your business.

Design brief — instructions to your agency/designer, focusing them on interpreting the core of your business.

Brand guidelines — the standard reference document where the elements above are written down to ensure consistency in all future applications.

business comes under the heading of brand strategy, a subject to which many books and articles have been devoted. But however your thinking about branding is dressed up, the key is to think clearly about what you do, and to connect the dots between how you see yourself and how your market sees you.

If you can pin down the essence of your business in a few words that make sense from the perspective of customers, suppliers and employees, then you have the building blocks of your brand. Talk with colleagues, with customers, friends and family; ask them what they think it is you do that's special. Remember you're not looking for a tagline for public consumption: It doesn't have to be polished, just true to what you are. Without being too rigid, you can use this phrase as a reference point against which any aspect of your business can be measured, from your choice in office refreshments through to how you chase late payers and everything in between. If it all more or less adds up, you're on your way to creating a brand.

When you're happy that you have arrived at a believable set of words that sum up how you do what you do, you can begin the process of

BELOW
McKeown recounts the heritage of the Poppy brand at the briefing, giving the agency a concise history from which they can begin to develop a new visual identity

ABOVE
McKeown feels it's time for a change. As the brand goes from strength to strength, she's confident that a design revamp will only help her succeed in growing the company further in the months and years to come

applying your brand. Of course, the first point of contact a brand has with the world is usually through its visual identity, so it's not surprising that most people start here; a good deal of effort and often expense can go into arriving at a logo design that fits the bill. But so long as you've done your homework and have an understanding of the essence of your business, this process can be stimulating and enjoyable, and the cost can be kept to a minimum.

Leslie McKeown owns Poppy, a boutique clothing store in Manhattan's Nolita neighborhood. Deciding that she could put her love of fashion to work, McKeown established her small business on the hunch that she could express and commercialize her distinctive vision for women's retailing. Like many start-ups, in the beginning McKeown got a friend to help with Poppy's visual identity, signage and packaging. The sense she wanted to put across was newness — designers, styles, cuts — before all else, and so a certain rough-around-the-edges feel was not only permissible, but welcome. McKeown used innovative, low-cost ideas that did a good job of communicating Poppy's cutting-edge status, and she gave thought to a persona for Poppy — "the

smartest girl you know" — expressing it in the range and pricing of her stock, as well as in the décor of the store itself.

Clearly she did something right, because Poppy's success is now an established fact: McKeown's customers keep coming back. They value her commitment to remain ahead of the curve, the risks she takes with new designers and the discernment she applies to the few vintage pieces the store carries. In the meantime, McKeown and her husband started a family, and her thoughts began to turn to the possibilities of new lines — babywear, perhaps — and to raising her sights in terms of challenging a new level of competition. She began to feel that although Poppy's original brand identity had been admirably suited to the job, she'd outgrown it, and that it was time to give it some fresh thought.

At growth points such as this, the services of an outside design agency can be particularly useful in helping you to express your extended ambitions. A good agency has the technical experience to provide you with a new brand identity that will grow with you and that can be produced in a variety of possibly unforeseen settings. They will also

THIS PAGE

*The presentation of both routes gets
a warm reception, with McKeown
visibly delighted at the results*

work with you to ensure that your identity continues to express what has made you successful to date, as well as embracing your new aspirations. In this way your existing customers will still recognize you even as you reach out to new audiences.

Hiring outside help comes with a cost, of course, and you'll want to be certain you're getting value for money. If you're starting out, there's every chance that your budget will direct you towards a freelancer. Happily, a lack of overhead doesn't equate with a lack of creativity: Many highly talented individuals simply choose to work this way. Ideally you'll find a supplier through word of mouth, but the Web presents a fantastic showcase for designers too (try *www.elance.com*). However, if you're growing and need to refresh or even re-brand your business, an investment in the broader experience of an agency may well make sense, because your existing brand values need to be protected as well as extended. How can you be sure you choose the right company or freelancer? A combination of recommendations, a realistic price point and track record should answer most of your concerns, but there are some good signs you

can glean from your first meeting with a prospective agency. Do you feel in control? Are your brand issues front and center in the meeting? If you're not subjected to endless case studies and a litany of proprietary formulas on "how we tackle branding," but instead are engaged in a thoughtful discussion about you, then you're probably on the right track.

McKeown chose to work on the new Poppy with a European design agency with offices in New York. A meeting with them left her impressed. "They were very respectful towards my intuitive understanding of what Poppy is all about, and helped me to find words for it — they didn't put them in my mouth." The agency was careful to ascertain whether there were likely to be any unusual applications of the new brand identity, and, sure enough, McKeown told them about an idea for little stickers to hold wrapping tissue in place.

The agency took over from there, and within a few days had narrowed their thinking down to two routes, each of which they felt expressed an aspect of the Poppy brand. Most agencies produce a number of designs, but in the end will present only the two or three that they feel most closely fit the requirement. You

THIS PAGE

Decisions, decisions —
McKeown must now take a few
days to reflect on both routes before
making a final commitment to a
new visual identity

should expect to see several treatments of the identity, in various colors and at various sizes, as well as in a variety of applications — business cards, compliments slips, etc. Additionally, a good designer will propose and supply you with a typeface for your brand, contributing further to distinctiveness in every aspect of its public appearance.

On the day of the presentation the agency kept an open mind, giving equal emphasis to the two design concepts they brought with them to show McKeown. Explaining how both approaches connected with the Poppy brand, they gave McKeown plenty of room to reflect on the implications that each might have for her business.

A SIMPLE SIX-STEP BREAKDOWN OF THE BARE ESSENTIALS

1. Are you certain about the foundations of your brand? Talk to people from all sides of your business, and from outside it, too, to see how their opinions measure up against yours. Your brand also lives in their eyes and minds, not just yours.

2. Try to arrive at a brief summary of your brand that truly represents what it is you're about. Remember it's not a tagline, but a set of standards and values against which all aspects of your business should measure up.

3. For your visual identity, whether you're just starting out or having a refresh,

decide if an independent freelancer or an agency is appropriate to your scale and inclination.

4. Talk to a few possible suppliers. Do they connect with your brand idea? Do they listen to you? Are they inspired by your brand? Are you inspired by them?

5. Expect to see two or three possible results. Be sure you factor in any special production costs as part of your decision.

6. Remember your new brand identity will need constant nourishment: Living your brand throughout your business will give it that.

ROUTE 1

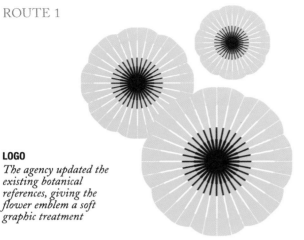

LOGO

The agency updated the existing botanical references, giving the flower emblem a soft graphic treatment

ABCDEFGHIJKLMNOPQRSTUVWXYZ
abcdefghijklmnopqrstuvwxyz
0123456789

**ABCDEFGHIJKLMNOPQRSTUVWXYZ
abcdefghijklmnopqrstuvwxyz
0123456789**

**ABCDEFGHIJKLMNOPQRSTUVWXYZ
abcdefghijklmnopqrstuvwxyz
0123456789**

LOGO VARIATIONS

The Poppy "flower" was combined with the logotype to be applied to all stationery and packaging collateral

COLOR PALETTE

Subtle shades of pink, blue and green reflect the botanical heritage and ethereal qualities of the brand

Poppy   281 Mott Street
        New York City 10012
        T: 212 219 8934
        F: 212 219 0620

Poppy
281 Mott Street, New York City 10012
T: 212 219 8934 F: 212 219 0620

TYPOGRAPHY

Three weights of the typeface, Clarendon, have been incorporated into the identity. This serif font is feminine, playful and works well across all communications

ROUTE 2

LOGO

Again, the flower design was employed as the logo in route two, but was rendered in a more graphic treatment, affording the brand an iconic visual mark

ABCDEFGHIKLMNOPQRSTUVWXYZ
abcdefghijklmnopqrstuvwxyz
0123456789

ABCDEFGHIKLMNOPQRSTUVWXYZ
abcdefghijklmnopqrstuvwxyz
0123456789

ABCDEFGHIKLMNOPQRSTUVWXYZ
abcdefghijklmnopqrstuvwxyz
0123456789

281 MOTT STREET
NEW YORK CITY 10012
T: 212 219 8934
F: 212 219 0620

TYPOGRAPHY

Helvetica Neue in three different weights is high on legibility and gives the brand a modern appearance. This sans serif font works well on both small and large applications

LOGO VARIATIONS

Linear and black and white block variations were mocked up to show McKeown how the logo could work in monotone applications

COLOR PALETTE

A strong color palette was developed in contrast to route 1's more subdued shades. Reds, blues, greens and ochres give the brand "pop"

A DECISION IS MADE

Having given careful consideration to both design directions, McKeown chose route one: "When I first laid eyes on the presentation it was like looking in the mirror. It was an amazing feeling to have someone nail my aesthetic so completely, and take it even further than I had considered.
It very much reaches in the direction I want to take Poppy — organic roots, but relentlessly modern in outlook. I can 'grow' with this look for a long time."

McKeown now has a tool kit to take her business to new heights. Clothes tags, stationery, and even a neat sticker seal and rubber stamp combination for the shopping bags have all been included in the comprehensive design package.

This is the sense *you* should get from a brand identity exercise, combining a mini-consultancy with the delivery of a tangible product you can use to take your business onwards and upwards.

COUNTING THE COST

Branding your business adds resilience and profitability to what you do. It's clearly worth your time and money to develop the brand most appropriate to your market, but, in the end, only you can judge how much to budget against doing so. The brand identity marketplace will undoubtedly rise to the challenge you present. However, as a rule of thumb, expect little for under $2,000, and for that price you'll need to deliver all of the strategic thought yourself. A good small agency may take on the job from around $10,000 (although a large international agency might charge much more, depending on their talent base and experience) and for this you can expect an active contribution to your thinking, challenging ideas and the delivery of production-ready assets. Never underestimate the rewards a well-conceived brand can bring in any business sector. Whether it's for an everyday purchase or a once-in-a-lifetime professional service, good branding communicates high quality, reliability and trust. And, as a brand owner, it builds long-term operational and balance-sheet-value in your business.

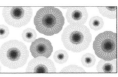

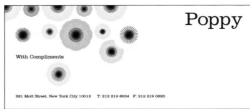

BUSINESS CARDS
Simple and legible, the Poppy business cards are given a colorful flower pattern on the back to reinforce the brand logo

SHOPPING BAGS
Large and small stickers have been designed to apply to the shopping bags. The smaller one acts as a seal on the handle to give a sense of secrecy and detail

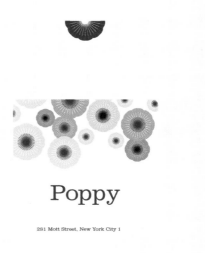

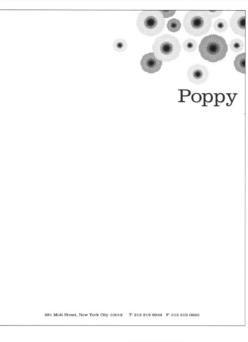

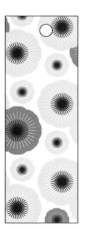

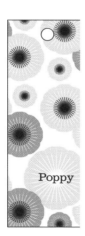

LETTERHEAD
The flower pattern is also applied to the letterhead to ensure continuity throughout the identity

SWING TAGS
A selection of swing tags in varied "Poppy" colors and designs will offer product standout and immediacy on the racks

QUESTIONS OF STYLE

— *I'm working to a tight budget. How do I prioritize the investment in the various components of my brand identity?*

First, invest your time in understanding what your brand is: If you need help, get it and pay for it if necessary. Then the next steps will be clear, leaving you to judge what can be achieved against available budget.

— *I've never cared about design. Why is brand identity so important to me?*

It provides your business with a foundation from which it can grow. Your identity is a shorthand that enables you to communicate the idea behind what you do efficiently and leaves you to get on with doing it!

— *So, what makes a strong brand identity?*

Relevance, clarity and consistency. The elegant expression of a clear business strategy will be attractive and inspire confidence. It should be flexible and relevant to customers wherever they experience it, from letterhead to telephone manner.

— *I have already built my brand. How do I update it without damaging it?*

You should seriously consider talking to a professional. Your brand may have grown in ways you don't directly appreciate, and impartial outside eyes will be able to recommend what you keep, what you build on and what you leave behind.

— *My business has few physical components on which to apply logos. Should I bother with branding?*

Every business in every industry can benefit from good design. It is the face of your company and reflects your business philosophy. Great design can distinguish you from the competition.

ALL ADS UP

OUR OWN ADVERTISING AUTHORITY, DIEGO SCOTTI, GIVES US A CRASH COURSE IN HOW TO MAKE IT IN MARKETING

Times have changed. Long gone are the days when all you needed to do to reach the biggest audience was buy three, two-minute ad spots during a major sporting event. Of course, if you can afford to do so, it's still one of the best attention-grabbing ad stunts, but not everyone has six- and seven-figure marketing budgets. Even the largest corporations with significant budgets find the quandary of how best to advertise their own products and services a real challenge. Advertising agencies now offer other new-fangled avenues to explore. In addition to advertising in print and on TV, sometimes the most effective means of reaching your audience are far from traditional.

The channels by which we communicate are forever changing and multiplying — the Internet in particular has revolutionized the way we communicate, not only between each other, but with our favorite companies. And choosing the most effective conduit down which to send your message is a tricky decision to make, especially if the money you're spending could be put to better use elsewhere. With that in mind, we have developed five clear-cut principles to which any company, large or small, can subscribe.

— AIM CAREFULLY

Identify the channels that work for you. A mistake that many businesses make is to take the machine gun approach, when a sharply focused single shot can be much more effective and efficient, not to mention less messy. In fact, unless you carefully consider your customer and know where to find them, it is unlikely you are reaching them at all — merely spending money without maximizing the returns. Ask your customers how they have heard about you, and apply what you can from their answers to reach new ones. For example, if you have been marketing your business on-line, but most of your customers have come through referrals from other customers, you should dial down your web presence and think of ways to encourage more referrals.

— EXPERIMENT WISELY

Each business and its customers are different, and it is not possible to give fool-proof advice on which channels are the best for everyone. It is fair to say, however, that small businesses do often share one thing: a limited budget. Rather than investing all your available funds in multiple placements for the

Name:	DIEGO SCOTTI
Job Title:	VICE PRESIDENT OF GLOBAL ADVERTISING
Joined:	1993
Responsibility:	DEVELOPING AND OVERSEEING ADVERTISING AND COMMUNICATIONS EFFORTS ACROSS BUSINESS UNITS AND GEOGRAPHIES

same advertisement, or one direct mail to all your customers, it's a good idea to hold back some resources to use for an alternative campaign. Send a piece of mail to only part of your population, or take an advertisement in one local media outlet, and wait to see the results before you take the full plunge.

— WORD OF MOUTH

Word of mouth has always been the most powerful form of advertising. While it can be difficult to quantify, it is a very effective medium. Couple that with the obvious cost benefits — in many cases it's free — and it's a very attractive marketing method. Press coverage is one way to spread the word at ground level, but it's not always so easy to come by good editorial. Try approaching local media outlets and trade journals as a first step, although if you have a very strong story, for example a new product launch, don't shy away from other publications. Most importantly, consider what is genuinely newsworthy. Aside from press, you can also provide incentives to your customers to spread the word about your business by offering finders-fees, product trials to pass around or postcards.

— LEVERAGING THE WEB

The Internet is a marvelous equalizer. It doesn't matter whether you're large or small, a supermarket with 300 branches or an organic grocer with one — you have the same chance to succeed. If you can spread the word effectively you have the opportunity to advertise your services to an international audience and generate their interest. Create reasons for your customers to keep returning to your site: Updated news, blogs, podcasts or special offers are just some of the many ways to do this.

— MONEY WELL SPENT

If you do want to create a traditional advertising campaign, then choosing the right agency to work with is paramount. Base your decision on the quality of their work and on shared philosophies. It's no good hiring the "coolest" agency in town if all they want to do is push your brand too far. Why not consider spreading your budget to other promotional platforms such as generating news articles or features in the press? If you can pump some money back into your business to boost the quality of your product, then that's a great story and something worth shouting about.

GREAT TIMING

BETTER TIME MANAGEMENT IS KEY TO GUARANTEEING A LESS STRESSFUL AND MORE PRODUCTIVE WORKING DAY

A growing number of authors and life coaches are making a full-time career out of advising us on how to sift schedules and sort priorities. With a view toward reorganizing our lives along more chronologically elegant lines, their prescriptions range from broad common sense to insistent micro-management of every detail of our days and nights. But what they all have in common is the noble goal of liberating us from the monstrous anxiety caused by what we believe we have yet to do in the face of overwhelming deadlines.

At its heart, the time management industry is selling you tools to redraw some of the boundaries that modern life seems to be intent on dissolving, especially the boundaries between what you feel you need to do and what you actually have to do. Worry and inefficiency feed on this overwhelming confusion, and the key to straightening out your priorities is to spend a few days keeping a close log of what you're doing, for how long, and — most importantly — how you are really feeling about it. Be certain to do this honestly and meticulously, and a pattern as unique and revealing as your fingerprint will begin to emerge.

With the facts laid out before you, you can begin to spot trends and tendencies with ease: Inadvisable moments of relaxation, unnecessary overexertion, groundless worry and inaccurate optimism are all exposed. Reflect on dead time, on wasted time and on productive time as they appear in your record, and begin the task of addressing, activity by activity, how you might tidy up a few things. Deciding which actions you could group together, or which you need not have done yourself — for whatever reason — can be a liberating first step to effective management of your time.

Of course, no matter how well you compensate for your strengths and weaknesses, circumstances will always intervene. However, you can contain some of the turbulence in a working day by applying simple rules to your use of e-mail chat and cell phone, allocating specific times when you won't let them interrupt you.

In the end, though, you can expect diminishing returns if you seek to systematize every moment of your day. A good portion of the undoubted wisdom of any book that claims it will change your life is simply irrelevant in many cases, and pursuing somebody else's vision in totality will at best confer only small

advantages. The roots of creative endeavor as it applies to your business, on which only you can draw, lie in the sudden connection of unexpected circumstances and ideas, often in an environment you don't completely control. So build a framework with your own or with others' ideas to make you work more effectively and feel better, but make sure it will support those precious insights that never arrive in an orderly way. Such insights are of disproportionate importance to how you continue to build your business.

FIVE TIME-SAVING TIPS:

1. **Stay ahead of the curve** — There's nothing quite like arriving prepared. By getting up just a little earlier, you can spend half an hour or so in the calm of the early morning thinking through what's coming up and how you're going to react. Doing so will pay dividends later.

2. **Manage your interruptions** — Assign an hour in the morning and an hour in the afternoon to dealing with your correspondence. Try switching off your e-mail program in between to avoid scratching the "send and receive" itch every five minutes. If you're not paid to be on call, put your cell phone on silent, and pick a time to return all your calls later in the day.

3. **Get out** — Never underestimate the power of managed disruption. A change of scene for half an hour — even if it's just a walk around the block — will give you a chance to take stock and marshal your thoughts.

4. **Design your own to-do list** — Rather than just enumerating all your outstanding tasks, add some analysis that will help you identify how you can best do what needs to be done. How long do you estimate each task will take? Can you be interrupted? Simple, personalized categories will help you to keep on top of things.

5. **Cat nap** — It may seem like an emergency measure, but when the chips are down you'll be surprised at how refreshing a few minutes of light sleep can be — certainly enough to get you through an intense patch. Science suggests that making it a regular feature in your life will enhance your performance — making sure you stay ahead of the curve for tomorrow!

GOING GLOBAL

WE VISIT AWARD-WINNING SWEDISH "EXPERIENCE" MAKERS, KNOCK, TO GET AN INTERNATIONAL PERSPECTIVE ON BEST WORKING PRACTICES, AND HOW SMALL CAN BE EFFECTIVE

Sometimes it really pays off to walk a mile in someone else's shoes. In this case, we walked a kilometer in someone else's snowboots. When we meet Jonas Pinzke, the Creative Director of Knock Communications, and J.C. Fantechi, the Business Development Director at Åkestam Holst, at our hotel in Sweden's capital, Stockholm, we order a glass or two of *glögg* (Swedish mulled wine) to chase away the chills. Outside, the late afternoon temperature is shivering somewhere below zero, the sun has set long ago, and the frost is already beginning to creep across the lawns in Berzelii Park opposite the hotel. We have arranged to meet Pinzke and Fantechi for an informal briefing that evening before we spend a day shadowing them across Stockholm.

Before us sit two trailblazers of the Scandinavian event-planning scene: One a stylish Swede with a straightforward conversational manner, the other an animated Italian-American who emigrated to Sweden eight years ago after stints in London and Milan. When we began our quest to find a suitable international company to profile, we set ourselves some criteria that would focus our search. We were particularly interested in finding

a business that was challenging the traditional practices of an established sector; would provide inspiration to any enterprise in any industry back home; and offer the opportunity to immerse ourselves in a foreign culture.

The Nordic regions have always been a hotbed of innovation, with global automotive, telecommunications, industrial design and pharmaceutical industries all heavily populated by pioneering Scandinavian companies. Even their everyday approach to working life and environment is admired and exported the world over. In the World Bank's report *Doing Business in 2006*, Norway, Finland, Denmark and Sweden all feature in the top 15 international countries for doing business, ahead of Germany and France. So, it was with some pride that the boys and girls at Knock extended an invitation for us to spend a day in the life of a Scandinavian events firm.

"We liken our company to the Swedish people — open-minded, welcoming and hard-working," says Pinzke, in an impeccable American accent. "It is our business to connect people." Knock was conceived 10 years ago in association with Stockholm-based advertising agency Åkestam Holst. Originally, Knock was

LEFT
As part of Absolut's Three Tracks campaign, Knock organized a silent concert where partygoers listened to music on custom headphones

BELOW LEFT
Volvo Cars trained and entertained over 6,000 of its dealers over nine weeks in the unique Volvo C30 space

BELOW
A traditional Swedish breakfast awaits workers in the informal kitchen every morning

formed as a traditional event-planning company, working with clients who were already on the agency's roster and who are still with Knock today. Knock has evolved over time, however, to become a "worldwide three-dimensional communications agency." As Fantechi explains: "We're not big on convoluted marketing speak like 'B2B' (business to business) or 'B2C' (business to consumer); if we were, we'd have to describe ourselves as 'P2P' — person to person. In other words, we connect brands and their customers on a personal level." Pinzke jumps in: "It should be sensual — as humans we communicate via taste, sight, smell, touch and sound. There's no reason why companies can't do the same."

With that in mind, they create customized experiences for international clients across a spectrum of industries. Through the medium of events, Knock brings brands to life — transforming them from ideas and images into real-life experiences. It may sound new-fangled, but it really does work. If you as a consumer are given the opportunity to interact with a company on a physical and emotional level then you're bound to feel something — more so than you would by simply watching an ad.

"We have turned predictable communications methods on their head," says Pinzke. "We are experimenting to give consumers something to get a kick out of. That's very rare nowadays."

Knock recently staged an event for Volvo Cars and Volvo C30 in Gothenburg in the south of Sweden to introduce the new C30 model to all 6,000 of their international dealers. Bucking the usual automotive trend of simply setting up a stage where the car could be viewed, Knock created an immersive space which was furnished with objects and film footage representing the interests of the target market. Thirty shipping containers were employed as walls for the space and the furniture was modern and white to contrast with the containers. They didn't even showcase the car. The idea was to have the evening's food revolve on a sushi belt, with products that represented the target market interspersed between the dishes. "Volvo decided that it was more important to educate the dealers about their potential audience, because those were the people they would have to sell to face-to-face," says Pinzke. "On an overall score of six, the dealers gave the event a 5.8 — taking into account the food, the music, the experience. Quite an achievement."

LEFT
*Knock's 12 employees
sit side by side in their
very Swedish open-plan
office space*

BELOW
*Employees hold informal
meetings all around the
agency during the day*

The following morning, we arrive at Knock's offices on Kungsgatan, a busy shopping street that runs between Norrmalm and Östermalm, the northern and eastern districts of the city. As we walk through the door of its fourth-floor office, we're welcomed into a very Swedish space populated by very Swedish staff. Knock shares its workspace with Åkestam Holst, so the atmosphere is abuzz with creative types sharing ideas in the open-plan office. We are met by Jonas Pinzke, who leads us past the Knock desks and into a homey kitchen, where he offers to prepare us coffee and a typical Swedish breakfast of fruit bread, cheese and caviar in a tube (it's a lot tastier than it sounds). We enjoy it in the company of a steady stream of employees who nip in and out to greet their workmates. We retire to the Knock lounge where Pinzke and the C.E.O. of the company, Jesper Kjærgaard, tell us more about the agency.

Today, there are 12 "Knockers," the same number of employees the group began with. The company's intention was never to grow, and in turn never to compromise the quality of their work. "We wanted everyone to be able to sit around an average-sized table so we all have

ABOVE LEFT
A shelf in the reception groans under the weight of the agency's trophies

LEFT
Knock in high spirits: an Absolut brainstorm

ABOVE
This open-plan kitchen acts as a sociable partition between the main office and the inspiration library

KNOCK'S BUSINESS PHILOSOPHY

1. **Keep it simple** — the best business is brilliantly conceptualized, and simply executed.

2. **Be unique, stay unique** — identify what you do that no one else in the market is doing.

3. **You are no better than your most recent job** — always strive for more.

4. **Mix your team, it's the differences that could bring you together** — consistently aim towards the multidimensional.

5. **Invest in your client, and the client will invest in you** — have a long-term perspective on your business.

an equal say. We'd be too big with any more than 12," insists Kjærgaard. It is this lack of compromise that characterizes Knock's approach and wins awards; in the reception area there is a shelf full of prizes ranging from American Clios to Cannes Lions. When we compliment the staff on the office design they tell us they remodeled it themselves two years ago. "Everything we do is consistent, from the furniture to the Web site; everything feels like it came from the same stable," says Pinzke.

With that, he invites us to sit in on an internal briefing meeting, which is for Absolut vodka. They set about brainstorming an event in their lilting Swedish tongue. We don't understand a word, but given the animated reactions and jovial discourse it must have been a resounding success. By the end of the morning we're ready for lunch. Kjærgaard's dog Spike joins us for sushi, but sneezes at the spicy wasabi, sending the team into fits of laughter. Several employees bring their dogs to work, which adds to the laid-back atmosphere around the office. It's certainly a place where you feel instantly at home — everyone seems to have struck that perfect balance between hard work and enjoyment.

Knock is in the process of organizing some events — or "experiences" — for a selection of clients, and days are currently spent dreaming up exciting situations, coordinating details and visiting possible venues. After lunch we head for the Luma Huset, a converted light bulb factory in the south of the city, which has an incredible glass structure perched on the roof. We spend some time at the top overlooking the whole of Stockholm, and the guys at Knock all agree it will make the perfect setting for one of their exclusive events. With another burst of energy we move swiftly from the factory to one of Stockholm's oldest and most revered restaurants, Teatergrillen. We are led through the old-world Italian dining room into the industrial kitchens where the linen-aproned staff are clearing up after the final lunch customers. More booming Scandinavian laughter and backslaps signal another successful meeting with one of the head chefs, and it's only then that we realize that it's well past the end of the working day and we're already late for our flight.

After many handshakes and more backslaps we head for the airport having spent an enjoyable day following Knock around their hometown. Sitting in the departures lounge at Arlanda, we realize that we'll miss the bright and airy Kungsgatan office, the inspiring staff who are more friendly than trendy, and the laid-back yet productive work ethic that infuses the company. We leave wishing that every workplace was a little more like this one — open-minded, industrious and a thoroughly enjoyable place to work. As for their philosophy, they've actually given it a name: "cocktail." The gist? That it's perfectly acceptable to mix in a lot of ingredients as long as you consider the end result and the taste of your drinker. They certainly mixed up a memorable visit for us.

SERVICE INCLUDED

JOHN STEWARD IMPARTS SOME USEFUL ADVICE ON HOW TO SERVE YOUR CUSTOMERS EFFICIENTLY AND WITH DIGNITY

So, the customer's always right. This universal consumer relations tenet is often viewed as a negative philosophy — a tired eye-roller among product and service providers. Some truisms stick for a reason, however, and companies who ignore the value of their customers' opinions are effectively committing commercial suicide. Those businesses that use their customers' comments as a foundation on which to build a better service are the ones who will survive. It is time companies embraced a more positive attitude, engaging customers in dialogue, and preventing an "us and them" situation.

Before we get to the nuts and bolts, an over-arching service philosophy is to consider short and long-term visions — evaluate what the customer can do for you in the long-term and take action accordingly in the short. Also, try not to let your customer service be ruled by your own policies. The more flexibility you can build into solving your customers' problems, the better you'll be able to serve them and the more content they are likely to be. By earning customers' trust you can anticipate and solve problems before they occur. Why not set a pattern for first experiences. Make the first impression the best you can, and in that way you will set the tone from that moment on. It will help to engage them from the start.

That said, there are plenty of ways in which you, as a small business owner, can build even better relationships with your customers, enabling you to care for their needs at every step. Take your servicing cues directly from them and serve your customers in the same way that you would expect to be served by any other business yourself. What follow are five rules of best practice when it comes to customer service.

—   LISTEN

The first step towards understanding the customer is to listen to them carefully. Often, the customer won't know the right question to ask and is simply frustrated by their own lack of knowledge. It is your job and the job of your employees to ask the right questions, evaluate the problem, and provide the customer with context. If you don't listen, you may misinterpret the issue at hand, and you will be unlikely to solve it. As a result, the customer will walk away even more frustrated than they were to start with.

Name:	JOHN STEWARD
Job Title:	SENIOR VICE-PRESIDENT, CHARGE & CUSTOMER RELATIONSHIP MANAGEMENT
Joined:	1987
Responsibility:	DIRECTS CUSTOMER RELATIONSHIP MANAGEMENT AND CUSTOMER LOYALTY STRATEGIES

— BE FLEXIBLE

Solving an issue requires flexibility, because not all customers' problems are the same. Companies should look at their business model and make proactive decisions about how they can be flexible and still compete. Customer issues can rarely be solved with a one-size-fits-all approach. However, you also can't be so flexible as to jeopardize your business. Rather, you need to stretch yourself to ensure flexibility in whatever area you can. Flexibility will allow you to be responsive to problems and solve them successfully.

— EMPOWER YOUR PEOPLE

Customers should never be forced to talk to several different people to get their questions answered. They must be able to call or interact at first contact and know that the issue has been taken care of on the spot, or the person they dealt with will work to solve it themselves. The more times a customer calls to have their issue solved, the more frustrated they will be and the poorer their view of the company. As a result, the person interacting with the customer must be empowered to make the decisions and take action. If, as a C.E.O., you do not have the time to solve all the problems, your employees must feel as though they are authorized.

— INCREASE ACCESSIBILITY

We all strive to offer the best products and services with the least amount of hassle, but there will be moments when customers will need to ask about something or complain. All businesses should be available in their customers' times of need, and specifically when their problems arise. No one should have to leave more than one message or be forced to wait days for an appropriate response.

— ENSURE CONSISTENCY

No matter what your business does, it is imperative to ensure that your service approach is kept consistent throughout the entire organization. Customers should be attended to with the same impeccable service attitude whether it is on the telephone, via the Internet or in person. All employees should understand the company's customer service ethos and be well trained as to how it should be implemented across the many facets of the business.

CONSCIENCE DECISION

THINK BEYOND JUST RECYCLING AND SAVING ELECTRICITY: TAKING STEPS TO PRESERVE THE ENVIRONMENT SAVES MONEY AND ALSO HELPS FUTURE-PROOF YOUR BUSINESS

Sustainability makes sense for the environment *and* for business. For the small business owner with tight margins, there are a multitude of benefits to adopting a more sustainable approach. For a start, streamlined processes, by their very nature, consume less time, resources and money, creating instant savings with a tangible effect on the bottom line. It's not just a case of making expensive investments — perhaps the biggest leap that exponents of sustainable working should make is to understand that, in the short term, the biggest savings are made by doing less, not more. In an age of fluctuating energy prices and long-term uncertainty, those with robust sustainability strategies will benefit most.

The workplace is often an energy-inefficient environment where consumables are thoughtlessly wasted or discarded. Yet energy is a commodity like any other; save it, and you save money. Cut costs, and you're not only improving your bottom line, but also contributing to reducing demand for energy and materials. No amount of gadgets, be they wind-up, solar-powered or low-energy, can equate to a simple strategy for cutting down on paper, toner, waste and other consumables.

If you don't want to keep new gadgets to a minimum, try to ensure that electronic equipment is as efficient as possible. The U.S. government's 1992 Energy Star program aimed to cut power consumption, and therefore carbon emissions, from electronic devices. The Environmental Protection Agency's 2004 report claims that the program shaved $10 billion from energy costs in the first 12 years of its life, and new, more stringent power management legislation debuts in 2007, in a bid to slash the vast amount of power drawn from devices left on stand-by — allegedly as high as 70 per cent.

According to the Environmental Protection Agency report, the U.S. market for environmentally friendly goods topped $10 billion in 2005 (double that of 2004) but the steady demand for electronics means carbon emissions are still rising. In the face of such rampant growth, many people are resigned to being unable to make any impact at all. But given that minimizing your environmental footprint is all about reducing costs, there are immediate benefits to be had from switching things off, conserving energy and making the most of available resources.

In the short-term, your energy-saving options are potentially endless. Almost every aspect of running a small business is an opportunity for positive change, whether in transportation, power consumption, recycling, streamlining business practices or even the very nature of your business itself. Here in the U.S., voluntary demand for renewable energy sources rose by over 1,000 per cent in the first five years of the 21st century, according to the U.S. Department of Energy's National Renewable Energy Laboratory — and other sectors are following suit. Although you may find the debate about global warming depressingly politicized, the sustainable path is a smart way to save money and grow your business. Most importantly, businesses are best placed to make the most of these opportunities, ensuring that consistent growth is achieved responsibly.

1. PERSONAL TRANSPORT

Transport is crucial for many small businesses, and the automobile is in no danger of being usurped. What has changed, however, is that businesses choosing the greener option often find themselves cutting costs as well as emissions. The most high-profile new technology is the hybrid drive car, which saves money on fuel and also cuts emissions. U.S. delivery companies are fast recognizing the suitability of hybrid electric vehicles for urban areas: Fed-Ex expects its OptiFleet E700 delivery truck to decrease particulate emissions by 96 per cent and reduce fuel costs by a third. Electric and hybrid cars have been at the forefront of the shift away from gasoline, with Toyota, Honda and Lexus leading the way in terms of sales and technological advancements. The eco-friendly luxury market is currently dominated by Lexus but will soon be joined by hybrid vehicles from Audi and Mercedes and a hydrogen-powered model from BMW. Dedicated electric vehicles continue to make great strides in terms of usability and can make the most sense in the urban environment, with Mitsubishi soon to offer an all-electric car. However, the last U.S. census reports that less than 0.5 per cent of Americans commute by bicycle, perhaps the most cost-effective and beneficial method of all.

— *Join a car-sharing organization and cut costs and parking dilemmas. CityCarShare, (citycarshare.org), in San Francisco, has special rates for employers.*

— *Start an office carpool; ensure that vehicles are properly maintained to assist efficiency.*
— *Assess your public transport options. In many cities it makes sound economic sense.*
— *Promote cycling. Introducing this kind of shift often needs a bit of encouragement — can bike users be rewarded for their choices?*
— *Take advantage of tax credits available — businesses that buy or lease an electric or hybrid car or truck are currently eligible for income tax credits up to $3,400 under the Energy Policy Act of 2005.*

2.   SAVING ENERGY

Despite a huge increase in the uptake of renewable energy, the U.S. still relies heavily on conventional energy-production methods. The Energy Information Administration reports that well over 50 per cent of all our oil is imported, often from unstable sources, leaving the economy increasingly at risk from fluctuations in the erratic geo-political situation. The cost of lighting, heating and cooling businesses will only increase, making the conservation of energy a sound business practice. Far-reaching, architecture-led approaches can slash energy use through design, though current conservation standards for new buildings don't necessarily go far enough. In addition, the vast majority of the country's workforce operates out of old buildings that don't meet strict regulation codes and are extremely uneconomical to adapt. Newer greener buildings make use of relatively simple design features to maximize natural light and ventilation, as well as bringing other benefits.

Sourcing cleaner energy is one way to offset the problems, but reducing overall energy consumption should be paramount.
— *Air-conditioning consumes vast quantities of energy, often needlessly. Chill less aggressively and stagger temperatures throughout the day.*
— *Drafts and solar gain cost money: Reduce energy costs by installing awnings to prevent over-heating in the summer and heavy curtains or weather-stripping to prevent drafts in the winter.*
— *Replace conventional 3.5-gallon toilet tanks with 1.6-gallon models or ultra-low-flow toilets. Or simply drop a brick in the cistern as an effective short-term measure.*
— *Again, look into the tax advantages available — reducing the energy consumption of a commercial building can make a business eligible for up to a 30 per cent tax credit, although this might only apply until the end of 2007.*

3.   CREATING ENERGY

Advances in small-scale energy generation are moving quickly. Wind turbines and solar panels are slowly becoming consumer products; the Alternative Energy Store (*home.altenergystore.com*) sells compact wind turbines and a range of solar panels to complement existing domestic boilers. Honda has been developing a "Home Energy Station" for the past few years; a compact fuel-cell generator system that will not only provide hydrogen for the next generation of fuel-cell cars, but also heating and hot water to a light-industrial property. The business applications of this are almost unlimited, providing low-cost energy as well as offering an essential back-up facility in the event of failure on the main power grid, such as the California blackouts of 2000.
— *Make the most of local conditions; is your environment suitable for wind energy applications: Is rainfall high enough to consider a storage tank?*
— *Combine resources wherever possible. Talk to other tenants in your building or plant about spreading the investment in an energy-generating infrastructure.*
— *Solar panels have come a long way. Look into new applications to meet your needs.*
— *Research business applications of home hydrogen filling stations to fill fuel-cell cars or solar-energy panels.*

4.   TECHNOLOGICAL SOLUTIONS

Recent studies indicate that up to 10 per cent of American residential electricity consumption is from devices left on stand-by. In the office environment, where PCs and lights often remain on overnight, this figure is probably far higher. States such as California have led the way in reducing power consumption, but simply turning off devices will have a noticeable effect; leaving a screensaver running makes no difference at all. While legislation ensures that power consumption levels fall in new devices, technological solutions can help lower the energy footprint of the typical office. The Palo Alto Research Center in California has been at the forefront of business technologies for the past few decades. It has developed "Clean Tech" products such as "transient paper," which uses inks that fade over a matter of hours allowing short-term print-outs to be reused. Although this process is still in prototype stage, it may one day replace printed pages. Wireless technology is a great boon to advocates of sustainable technology, allowing existing infrastructure to be upgraded with minimum waste.

— *Do you really need that company-wide PC upgrade? A new generation of online business tools, such as Linux* (linux.org) *can also help minimize the need for more hardware.*
— *Cutting-edge doesn't always mean high performance. Rethinking tried and tested technology can often make considerable financial and environmental savings.*
— *Where possible, reuse paper in printers and photocopiers; install storage bins for sheets to recycle and sheets to reuse. Companies such as Toshiba and Epson have launched free send-back programs, so you don't even pay for shipping.*

5.   SUSTAINABLE / RECYCLABLE PRODUCTS

The office environment offers a host of opportunities to reduce the materials footprint. For example, high oil prices have seen an increasing parity between the cost of virgin plastic packaging and the more expensive recycled alternatives. Many businesses, both large and small, are taking tentative steps towards the widespread use of recyclable packaging material. The market for goods and products made from recycled raw materials has exploded in the past decade, moving into the mainstream as designers and engineers raise the profile of recycled products. Companies such as Ecowork create conventional office furniture using recycled materials such as rubber, plastic, newsprint and cardboard. Manufacturers including IBM are experimenting with the use of 100 per cent-recycled materials, and although they are still in the prototype stage, the hope is that these swiftly decomposing products will avoid clogging up landfill with the detritus of our rampantly consumerist age.

— *As well as recycling, investigate materials-exchange schemes. Could shredded paper be reused as packing material?*
— *Use ceramic cups instead of paper or plastic ones.*
— *When equipment is reaching the end of its useful working life, consider donating it to charities or schools – you may even be able to claim a tax write-off.*

6.   SUSTAINABLE BUSINESS

Finally, expanding into sectors that impact directly on the demand for sustainable goods and services may be a shrewd financial move for your business as well. This is a major growth area, which one can expect to be bolstered by legislation even more in coming years. As consumers gain awareness of the issues, sustainable options are increasingly popular over their more wasteful counterparts (provided product quality is not compromised); all-natural cosmetics and organic foods are just the beginning. Right along the supply chain there are opportunities to pre-empt demand where it may not already exist, to innovate and ultimately take advantage of the movement.

— *Support local green business initiatives wherever possible, be it maintenance, production or partnerships.*
— *Many states are actively seeking investment from "green" businesses. Michigan, for example, is nurturing growth in sustainable areas through investment and promotion.*
— *Environment taxes are set to become part of everyday life, and preemptive business models which strive to avoid this additional tax will gain an undoubted commercial advantage.*
— *Remember that the advantages of locally -sourced materials far outweigh those of materials shipped long-distance.*

MARKET FORCES

CHELSEA MARKET WAS STARTED BY NEW YORK VISIONARY IRWIN COHEN. A DECADE LATER, HE REFLECTS ON SUCCESS WITH ONE OF THE MARKET'S FOUNDING BUSINESSES

Irwin Cohen is a property developer who believes that small businesses, not Madison Avenue and Wall Street, define the character of his hometown, New York City. So in 1994 he bought a 19th-century cookie factory in the dilapidated Chelsea section and turned it into Chelsea Market, a successful indoor market featuring specialty shops such as Amy's Bread and Frank's Butcher Shop. Those mom and pop businesses, in turn, attracted glitzy media properties such as the Food Network and Oxygen Media, which now occupy the second floor.

One of Cohen's first tenants was the Lobster Place, a wholesale and retail operation that today supplies Manhattan's most elite restaurants and has nearly doubled its revenue since 2002. That's when Ian MacGregor, 31, took over operations from his parents. "If we hadn't come here, the Lobster Place would have definitely gone out of business," says MacGregor.

Recently, Chelsea Market founder Irwin and Ian sat down in the seafood emporium to discuss their relationship and the secrets to transcending the tensions between landlord and tenant.

Irwin: I don't know if you know this, Ian, but I met your father about 12 years ago. How old were you then?

Ian: Let's see, I was 19.

Irwin: Right, you were in college, at the Coast Guard Academy, and I walked up to your father's store, right across the street here, and asked him, "What do you do?" I never knew lobsters were sold in New York City! I used to have to go up to Ogunquit, Maine, and load up the car. Later, I came up with the idea of creating a wholesale/retail market in this building. It used to be a very dangerous neighborhood — remember it?

Ian: The Canadian truck drivers who were delivering lobsters thought it was a no-man's land.

Irwin: If a driver got out to unload the back of the truck, someone would jump in and drive away — steal the truck! Anyway, when I got the idea for the Chelsea Market, I asked your father to join us.

Text: **Paul Keegan**
Photography: **Rainer Hosch**

PICTURED

Irwin and Ian discuss the changes to the area surrounding Chelsea Market in the Lobster Place, one of the first businesses to occupy the space

"Open a retail store?" he said, "you're crazy. It's not going to work." I told your father, "I know you're a wholesaler, but I want you to be a retailer, too." That was my plan. To be a tenant here, you had to be both.

Ian: Well, he used to be a retailer. And it worked out great. The truth is that for both our wholesale or retail businesses, as a stand-alone, neither is that great a business model. Because you're dealing with perishables. But what's great about Chelsea Market is that by marrying the two, you make each division much stronger.

Irwin: You seem to be taking the business from strength to strength. What's your secret?

Ian: Wish I knew — I'd write a book and make a lot of money. Well, in 2004, we automated the entire operation, so that really increased our capacity to do business. Our rent has stayed stable — that's been key. We signed a 20-year lease, so we have 10 years to go. We vastly increased our fish business because, with lobsters, you have to keep them alive, which cuts into your margin each time one dies. And the amount of traffic here has grown a great deal with the arrival of the Food Network in 2004.

Irwin: Well, what's good for the tenants is also good for the landlords. The building is still full and there's a waiting list of people who want to move in.

Ian: From day one, you had a vision and have taken a real genuine interest in our success. You walked into my father's old place across the street, and my father said, "I don't have money to build out or move my operation." And you said, "I'll lend you the money, don't worry about it." That's a dream landlord-tenant relationship.

Irwin: First of all, this was a social experiment for me. No one has ever done this. I'm not a retailer,

Irwin	I'm a lawyer. But I had this dream. I didn't meet the tenants through real estate brokers. I went out and personally found each one, and I sat in on all the negotiations, and made sure the lawyers did not behave inappropriately. I said these people are human beings and they have to be treated as such. My office was in the middle of this market and I had a table and sat right in the front window. Every tenant who walked by I spoke to, every day. All the tenants had my home phone number. And I said if something is not taken care of within five minutes, call me. I never got a phone call at home.
Ian:	And the customers are so important.
Irwin:	You learn so much from them. This is a real neighborhood, and that's what we need more of in New York. You hear about the big businesses that do so well, but it's actually the small businesses who buy from them. New York

survives because it's a small business environment. And as we keep these small businesses in Manhattan, we keep the character. I've lived in New York my whole life and the small businesses are what keep neighborhoods alive. That's what we've done here. Created a neighborhood. It really charges up my juices to see customers happy and to see people like you, and your mom and dad when they were here, running their businesses.

Ian: So what's your encore?

Irwin: The Bronx does not have very good food available for the population — there are no supermarkets up there — so I'm working on a plan now to take unused apartment buildings there and build family business enterprises, like you see here. What about you — what's next?

Ian: We'll be developing our online business to reach other

customers. With the exposure we get on the Food Network, there's an entire market in the West and Midwest that doesn't have any access to the products we sell, and we'd like to start reaching out to them.

Irwin: Well, you have matured this business to a point where I would put you up against any company in the fish business, anywhere. And I remember the day your father told me you were coming in to take over the business — at the time, you were in the Coast Guard, serving on an interdiction ship in Florida, chasing drug dealers!

Ian: That's right. But so much of our success has to do with where we are — here in the Chelsea Market. That's certainly why our business model works so well.

Irwin: You mean this is more fun than chasing drug dealers?

Ian: [*laughing*] Certainly less dangerous.

CHELSEA MARKET
75 Ninth Ave, New York, NY 10011
(212) 243-6005
www.chelseamarket.com

THE LOBSTER PLACE
436 West 16th Street, New York, NY 10011
(212) 255-5672
www.lobsterplace.com

OPEN FOR BUSINESS

SOME SAY SMALL BUSINESS IS THE NEW "BIG" BUT FROM OUR PERSPECTIVE, IT ALWAYS HAS BEEN. THE PROOF ISN'T JUST IN THE FACTS, BUT THE PLACE IT HOLDS IN OUR CULTURE

The inspiration for OPEN — the dedicated team at American Express that serves small businesses — is its customers, and the passion, dedication and resourcefulness with which they run their companies. These traits truly embody the entrepreneurial spirit, and are those upon which our country was founded. It is no surprise, then, that the term "entrepreneur" has become synonymous with the small business owner, or that these entrepreneurs hold an esteemed place in our culture.

Twenty years ago, American Express was among the first corporations to recognize these unique traits — and the very real needs — of entrepreneurs. The company has since evolved its products and services to reflect the best of the customers it serves and to provide them with the best means available to grow and market their businesses. Today, small businesses comprise one of the fastest growing areas of the economy. But the story did not begin a mere 20 years ago: Small businesses, and the entrepreneurs that run them, hold a very significant place in our history and society. Their story is reflected in our economy and our culture, and is one that we believe deserves its own celebration.

SMALL BUSINESS IS BIG

By the numbers, there's no question: Small business is the driving force of our economy and a fundamental contributor to America's wealth. Small businesses comprise 99.7 per cent of all businesses in the U.S.; they're responsible for half of our gross domestic product and they generate nearly 70 per cent of all new jobs.

But small business in the United States represents much more than a mere set of facts and figures. It holds a highly esteemed, almost mythical place in our culture. Indeed, the entrepreneurial spirit represents a founding ideal that underpins our entire nation: the idea that an individual should be free to pursue his or her own vision and passions.

Small business jump-started the modern economy, from the farmer working his small plot of land, to the proprietor of the local corner-store. And entrepreneurs have been at the very crux of many scientific or technological advances in recent history: the assembly line, the advent of electricity and telephones, the growth of the rail and airline industries. They were thinking outside of the box long before the term was coined.

Illustration: **Neal Whittington**

57% OF SMALL BUSINESSES ARE HOME BASED

Each year there are 1,000,000 new business start-ups

40,000,000

home businesses in the United States

Small businesses register 13-14 times more patents than any other sector

Small businesses are responsible for half of America's GDP — nearly $6 trillion annually

10.4 million small businesses in the U.S. are owned by women

72% of women in the workforce have children

86% of small business owners have taken steps to make their company more environmentally friendly

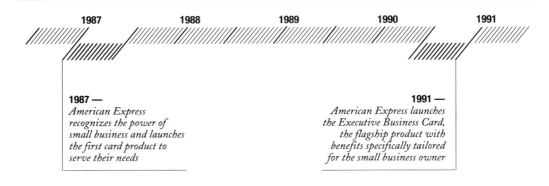

1987 —
American Express recognizes the power of small business and launches the first card product to serve their needs

1991 —
American Express launches the Executive Business Card, the flagship product with benefits specifically tailored for the small business owner

And small businesses are admired for reasons other than their concrete achievements: their resilience, their ability to adapt and take risks, their facility to succeed even when facing the most daunting challenge. The environment for small business has sometimes been far from friendly. The rise of corporate multinationals and other forms of "big business" meant that small businesses had to confront a new and powerful form of competition. In the decades following the birth of big business, small businesses also faced economic recessions, wars and eras of social transformation without the stability or resources of a larger corporation. Yet they continued to prosper and according to *U.S. News and World Report* grew at a rate of more than 200,000 per year.

THE NEW E-CONOMY

Recent years have provided a shining example of small businesses' enduring capacity to leave their larger rivals at the starting gate. With the advent of the personal computer, the Internet and e-commerce, entrepreneurship in the U.S. has undergone a "virtual" renaissance. There are few episodes in our business history to rival the paradigm shift heralded by the arrival of the likes of Amazon, Google and YouTube. That a relative upstart like AOL should see its name grafted onto the venerable Time Warner brand is unprecedented, and just one of the more overt signs of the enormous changes wrought by the innovators who first spotted the potential of the Internet.

These advances in technology level the playing field such that all businesses, whether small or big, reach their end customer through the same portal. The scales have been tipped in the direction of small business as traditional strengths like agility, flexibility and speed to market become the keys to success. In an era of "mass customization," big business can only look on while their nimble counterparts provide a quick and personalized service to their impeccably researched demographic. In fact, small businesses' mould-breaking structures and flatter hierarchies are revolutionizing the economy from the ground up. Never before have we seen small businesses spur entire industries, such as venture capital or angel investing, or witnessed the growth of sites like eBay, exclusively focused on providing a marketing platform for small businesses.

1992   1993   1994   1995   1996

1993 —
American Express dedicates full resources to a new Small Business Division, including trained service representatives who can offer specialized support to small business customers

1996 —
American Express provides small business owners with unsecured lines of credit of up to $50,000 as a source of funds when needed

66% of small business owners have a positive outlook on business growth

71% of small business owners offer healthcare benefits to employees

86% of small business owners have taken steps to make their business more environmentally friendly

70% of small business owners would recommend a friend or family go into business for themselves

Source: OPEN from American Express® Small Business Monitor

THE MELTING POT

Currently, over 650,000 new businesses are started yearly, according to the Small Business Administration. And, for the first time, those owned by women or minorities are outstripping all other categories. Women-owned firms alone total 10.4 million, employ more than 12.8 million people and generate $1.9 trillion in sales annually, reports the Center for Women's Business Research.

The explosion in small business creation has also inspired many who are new to the country to join the start-up revolution. The U.S. Hispanic Chamber of Commerce has found that Latino-owned businesses are growing at the fastest rate of any small business segment. This rise mirrors the increased spending power of the Hispanic consumer; in fact, 66 per cent of the most successful Hispanic-owned firms are small businesses, with growth rates at an enviable annual average of 17 per cent, as stated by *Hispanic Magazine*.

If small businesses are springing up everywhere, it's because there has never been a more providential time to start that start-up. Widespread PC ownership is key: It enables us

1997   1998   1999   2000   2001

1999 —
*American Express renames its Small Business
Division. It is now known as OPEN. New
services such as online and downloadable account
statements are also launched to help entrepreneurs
work more efficiently in the digital age*

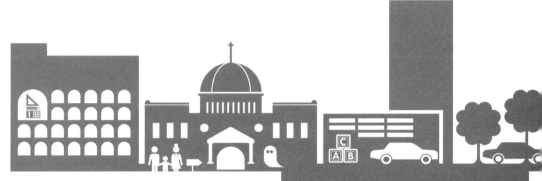

to start businesses in our kitchens or garages
with just a computer and a couple of thousand
dollars. In fact, according to SCORE:
Counselors to America's Small Business,
the number of small-office or home-office
businesses is now 40 million strong in the
U.S. — and growing at a viral rate of one
million each year.

And, as job security becomes a thing of
the past, many of these home-based businesses
are a seeding ground for another new type of
small business owner: the "mompreneur."
With 72 per cent of women with children now
participating in the workforce (up from only
47 per cent in 1975, according to the Bureau of
Labor Statistics), more and more mothers are
looking for ways to meld their professional and
personal lives, and see small business
ownership as the perfect vehicle. Joining them
are downsizing executives, trading the
corporate treadmill for something that they
own themselves and feel passionate about.

With this tectonic shift in work
practices, it's not surprising that economists
and policymakers are heralding a New
Economy based on technology, competition
and the ability to corner a niche in an

LOOKING TOWARDS 2017

The new "digital generation" are the
first to have grown up in a digital- and
internet-driven world giving rise to a
unique skill set that is informed by
hyper-mobility. They, more than any
other generation, will be able to create
companies in less time and with less
money and effort. Belmont University's
Jeff Cornwall reports that the
opportunities created by digital
technologies combined with this group's
willingness to take risks and be masters of
their own destiny will create the most
entrepreneurial generation yet.

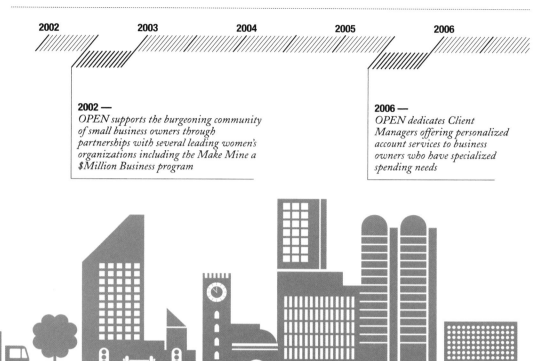

2002 — 2003 — 2004 — 2005 — 2006

2002 —
OPEN supports the burgeoning community of small business owners through partnerships with several leading women's organizations including the Make Mine a $Million Business program

2006 —
OPEN dedicates Client Managers offering personalized account services to business owners who have specialized spending needs

increasingly global marketplace. According to the Cato Institute, small businesses are paving the way in this altered landscape. They produce 13 to 14 times the number of patents as their larger counterparts, and comprise 97 per cent of America's exporters. In fact, 26 per cent of our export value is derived from goods and services produced by small business owners, according to the United States Small Business Administration. It is probably not a wild coincidence that the Ewing Marion Kauffman Foundation has discovered that states such as California, Massachusetts and Washington — all at the cutting edge of technological innovation — are also leading states for rates of entrepreneurship and small business.

THE FUTURE IS SMALL

Such a dramatic upswing in start-ups and changes in the basis of our economy may help small business to thrive, but it also means that small business owners face a very different set of challenges to those of a decade or two ago. The pace of technological innovation is astonishing, and small business owners have to think on their feet faster than ever before and

be ready to take advantage of opportunities as quickly as they present themselves. In order to innovate, they need access to state-of-the-art technology. To be globally competitive, they must be able to take advantage of supportive policies and infrastructure.

But amid all the changes and challenges, one thing remains true: the entrepreneurial spirit continues to thrive. Passion is the energy source that drives the business — from the original idea behind the enterprise to the persuasive way it is sold. It is their savvy that allows entrepreneurs to make the most of what they have and to get what they need.

At the close of this OPEN Book, we can only speculate about what the world will bring us in the next 20 years. In 1987, the Internet was in its infancy, and cell phones were the size of bricks. In 2027, will we be taking the likes of energy-harvesting floors, smart elevators and web-based microfinancing for granted? Whatever happens, two things are certain: Small businesses will continue their role as engines for innovation and exemplars of individualism for our economy, and OPEN from American Express will be doing all we can to help them achieve success.

OPEN frequently features our small business
customers in marketing and advertising, for
the media, and also with our internal team to
get a closer understanding of your experiences.

We invite you to share your business story with
us and want to hear about how you got started,
significant milestones, your products and
services, or even your experiences with OPEN.
OPENForum.com is our new online portal
that provides resources and the ability to
connect with other entrepreneurs to help you
grow your business. To share your story, please
visit us at:

www.OPENForum.com

To inquire about our products,
please call 1-800-NOW-OPEN.

For Customer Service, please call the number
on the back of your card.

OPEN BOOK is printed by:
American Express Publishing, Custom Solutions
1120 Avenue of the Americas
New York NY 10036

The text paper has been manufactured by
Mohawk using wind-generated electricity.